Kaplan Publishing are constantly finding new ways t̶ ̶ ̶ke a
difference to your studies and our exciting onlin̶ ̶ s really do
offer something different to students lookir̶ ̶ ̶ess.

This book comes with free MyKap̶' ̶ ̶ou can
study anytime, anywhere. **This**
separately and is included in t̶ **.d**

Having purchased this book, you have access to the following materials:

CONTENT	ACCA (including FBT, FMA, FFA)		FIA (excluding FBT, FMA, FFA)	
	Text	Kit	Text	Kit
Electronic version of the book	✓	✓	✓	✓
Knowledge checks with instant answers	✓		✓	
Material updates	✓	✓	✓	✓
Latest official ACCA exam questions*		✓		
Pocket Notes (digital copy)	✓		✓	
Study Planner	✓			
Progress Test including questions and answers	✓		✓	
Syllabus recap Videos		✓		✓
Revision Planner		✓		✓
Question Debrief and Walkthrough Videos		✓		
Mock Exam including questions and answers		✓		

* Excludes BT, MA, FA, FBT, FMA, FFA; for all other papers includes a selection of questions, as released by ACCA

How to access your online resources

Received this book as part of your Kaplan course?
If you have a MyKaplan account, your full online resources will be added automatically, in line with the information in your course confirmation email. If you've not used MyKaplan before, you'll be sent an activation email once your resources are ready.

Bought your book from Kaplan?
We'll automatically add your online resources to your MyKaplan account. If you've not used MyKaplan before, you'll be sent an activation email.

Bought your book from elsewhere?
Go to **www.mykaplan.co.uk/add-online-resources**
Enter the ISBN number found on the title page and back cover of this book.
Add the unique pass key number contained in the scratch panel below.
You may be required to enter additional information during this process to set up or confirm your account details.

This code can only be used once for the registration of this book online. This registration and your online content will expire when the examinations covered by this book have taken place. Please allow one hour from the time you submit your book details for us to process your request.

Please scratch the film to access your unique code.

Please be aware that this code is case-sensitive and you will need to include the dashes within the passcode, but not when entering the ISBN.

KAPLAN

PUBLISHING

ACCA Diploma in Financial and Management Accounting (RQF Level 2)

FA1

Recording Financial Transactions

EXAM KIT

KAPLAN

PUBLISHING

British Library Cataloguing-in-Publication Data

A catalogue record for this book is available from the British Library.

Published by Kaplan Publishing UK

Unit 2 The Business Centre

Molly Millar's Lane

Wokingham

Berkshire

RG41 2QZ

ISBN: 978-1-83996-375-9

Acknowledgements

These materials are reviewed by the ACCA examining team. The objective of the review is to ensure that the material properly covers the syllabus and study guide outcomes, used by the examining team in setting the exams, in the appropriate breadth and depth. The review does not ensure that every eventuality, combination or application of examinable topics is addressed by the ACCA Approved Content. Nor does the review comprise a detailed technical check of the content as the Approved Content Provider has its own quality assurance processes in place in this respect.

This product contains material that is ©Financial Reporting Council Ltd (FRC). Adapted and reproduced with the kind permission of the Financial Reporting Council. All rights reserved. For further information, please visit www.frc.org.uk or call +44 (0)20 7492 2300.

We are grateful to the Association of Chartered Certified Accountants for the permission to reproduce past examination questions. The answers have been prepared by Kaplan Publishing.

INTRODUCTION

Packed with practice and exam-type questions, this book will help you to successfully prepare for your exam.

- All questions are grouped by syllabus topics with separate sections for 'study support questions' (Section 1 of this book) and 'multiple choice questions' (Section 2).

- The study support questions (in section 1) are designed to test your understanding of the syllabus topics. These can be attempted either during your initial study or your early revision phase. In the approach to the exam you should turn your focus away from these to the exam style multiple-choice questions to gain exam practice.

- The multiple choice questions (in section 2) are all in exam style and of exam standard. You should ensure that in the last few days/weeks of your preparation before the exam you focus exclusively on this style of question to ensure you are sufficiently rehearsed in this style of question.

- A mock exam is provided at the back of the book. You should try this under timed conditions and this will give you an idea of how you will perform in your exam.

ENHANCEMENTS

We have added the following enhancement to the answers in this exam kit:

Tutorial note

Some answers include tutorial notes to explain some of the technical points in more detail.

CONTENTS

Quality and accuracy are of the utmost importance to us so if you spot an error in any of our products, please send an email to mykaplanreporting@kaplan.com with full details.

Our Quality Co-ordinator will work with our technical team to verify the error and take action to ensure it is corrected in future editions.

INDEX TO QUESTIONS AND ANSWERS

SYLLABUS AND REVISION GUIDANCE

SYLLABUS CONTENT

A   TYPES OF BUSINESS TRANSACTION AND DOCUMENTATION

1   Types of business transaction

(a)   Understand a range of business transactions including: (i)sales, (ii) purchases, (iii) receipts, (iv), payments, (v), petty cash, (vi) payroll.

(b)   Understand the various types of discount including where applicable the effect that trade discounts have on sales tax.

(c)   Describe the processing and security procedures relating to the use of: (i) cash, (ii) cheques, (iii) credit and debit cards, (iv) digital payment methods.

2   Types of business documentation

(a)   Outline the purpose and content of a range of business documents to include but not limited to: (i) sales invoice, (ii) supplier (purchase) invoice, (iii), credit note, (iv) debit note, (v), delivery note, (vi), remittance advice.

(b)   Prepare the financial documents to be sent to credit customers including: (i) sales invoice, (ii) credit note, (iii) statements of account.

(c)   Prepare remittance advices to accompany payments to suppliers.

(d)   Prepare a petty cash voucher including the sales tax element of an expense when presented with an inclusive amount.

3   Process of recording business transactions within the accounting system

(a)   Identify the characteristics of accounting data and the sources of accounting data records, showing understanding of how the accounting data and records meet the business' requirements.

(b)   Describe the key features of a computerised accounting system, including the use of external servers to store data (the cloud).

(c)   Summarise how users locate, display and check accounting data to meet user requirements and understand how data entry errors are dealt with.

(d)   Summarise the tools and techniques used to process accounting transactions and period-end routines and consider how errors are identified and dealt with the tools and techniques used to process accounting transactions and period-end routines and consider how errors are identified and dealt with.

(e)   Identify risks to data security, data protection procedures and the storage of data.

(f)   Explain the principles of coding in entering accounting transactions including: (i) describing the need for a coding system for financial transactions within a double entry bookkeeping system, (ii) describing the use of a coding system within an accounting system.

(g)   Code sales invoices, supplier invoices and credit notes ready for entry into the accounting system.

(h)   Describe the accounting documents and management reports produced by computerised accounting systems and understand the link between the accounting system and other systems in the business.

B   DUALITY OF TRANSACTIONS AND THE DOUBLE ENTRY SYSTEM

1   Double entry system

(a)   Define the accounting equation.

(b)   Demonstrate the use of the accounting equation.

(c)   Describe how the accounting equation relates to the double entry bookkeeping system.

(d)   Explain how transactions are entered into the accounting system.

2   Journal entries

(a)   Explain the use of journal entries including the reasons for and format of journal entries.

(b)   Prepare journal entries for various transactions.

3   Elements of the financial statements

(a)   Define and distinguish between the elements of the financial statements.

(b)   Identify the content of a statement of financial position and statement of profit or loss and other comprehensive income.

C   BANK SYSTEM AND TRANSACTIONS

1   The banking process

(a)   Explain the differences between the services offered by banks other financial services businesses.

(b)   Describe how the bank clearing system works.

(c)   Identify and compare different forms of payment.

(d)   Summarise the processing and security procedures relating to the use of cash, cheques, credit cards, debit cards and digital payment methods.

2   Documentation

(a)   Explain why it is important for an organisation to have a formal document retention policy.

(b)   Identify the different categories of documents that may be stored as part of a document retention policy.

D PAYROLL

1 Process payroll transactions within the accounting system

(a) Calculate and prepare entries in the accounting system to process payroll transactions including: (i) calculation of gross wages for employees paid by the hour, paid by output and salaried workers, (ii) accounting for payroll costs and deductions, (iii) the employer's responsibilities for taxes, state benefit contributions and other deductions.

(b) Identify the different payment methods in a payroll system, e.g. cash, cheques, automated payments.

(c) Explain why authorisation of payroll transactions and security of payroll information is important in an organisation.

E GENERAL LEDGER ACCOUNTS

1 Prepare general ledger accounts

(a) Prepare general ledger accounts clearly showing the balances brought forward and carried forward as appropriate.

F CASH AND BANK

1 Maintaining cash records

(a) Record cash transactions within the accounting system, including any sales tax effect where applicable.

2 Maintaining a petty cash record

(a) Enter and analyse petty cash transactions in the accounting system including any sales tax effect where applicable.

(b) Demonstrate the use of the imprest and non-imprest systems of maintaining a petty cash record.

(c) Reconcile the petty cash record with cash in hand.

(d) Prepare and account for petty cash reimbursements.

G SALES AND CREDIT TRANSACTIONS

1 Recording sales, customer account balances and trade receivables

(a) Record sales transactions taking into account: (i) various types of discount, (ii) sales tax, (iii) the impact of the sales tax ledger account where applicable.

(b) Enter sales invoices and credit notes issued to customers into the accounting system.

(c) Prepare the trade receivables general ledger account by accounting for: (i) Sales (ii) Sales returns, (iii) Receipts from customers including checking the accuracy and validity of receipts against relevant supporting information (iv) Discounts (v) Contra entries.

(d) Prepare entries in the accounting system to record cash sales, credit sales and receipts from customers.

(e) Account for irrecoverable debts and allowances for irrecoverable debts.

H   PURCHASES AND CREDIT TRANSACTIONS

1   Recording purchases, supplier account balances and trade payables

(a)   Record purchase transactions taking into account: (i) various types of discounts, (ii) sales tax, (iii) the impact of the sales tax ledger account where applicable.

(b)   Enter supplier invoices and credit notes received from suppliers into the accounting system.

(c)   Prepare the trade payables general ledger account by accounting for: (i) purchases, (ii) purchase returns, (iii) payments to suppliers including checking the accuracy and validity of the payment against relevant supporting information, (iv) discounts, (v) contra entries.

(d)   Prepare entries in the accounting system to record cash purchases, credit purchases and payments to suppliers.

I   RECONCILIATIONS

1   Purpose of reconciliations

(a)   Describe the purpose of reconciliations to external documents as a checking device to aid management and help identify errors.

(b)   Explain why it is important to reconcile to external documents regularly and to deal with discrepancies quickly and professionally.

2   Reconcile the cash records

(a)   Reconcile the cash records to a bank statement and deal with any discrepancies.

3   Reconcile individual supplier accounts

(a)   Reconcile the balances on individual supplier accounts to supplier statements and deal with any discrepancies.

J   PREPARING THE TRIAL BALANCE

1   Prepare the trial balance

(a)   Extract an initial trial balance.

2   Correcting errors

(a)   Identify types of errors that are revealed by extracting a trial balance.

(b)   Identify types of errors that are not revealed by extracting a trial balance.

(c)   Prepare journal entries to correct errors in the trial balance.

(d)   Identify when a suspense account is required and clear the suspense account using journal entries.

(e)   Redraft the trial balance following correction of all errors.

PLANNING YOUR REVISION

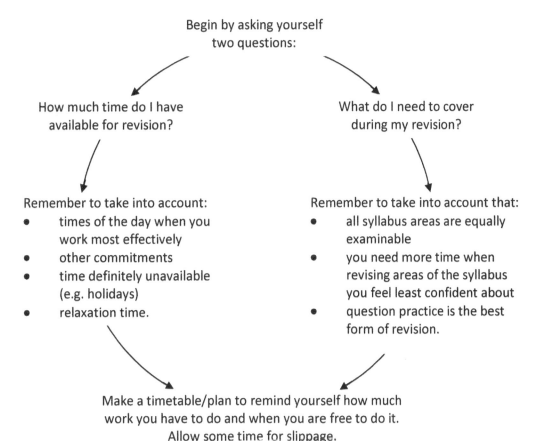

Begin by asking yourself
two questions:

How much time do I have
available for revision?

What do I need to cover
during my revision?

Remember to take into account:
- times of the day when you work most effectively
- other commitments
- time definitely unavailable (e.g. holidays)
- relaxation time.

Remember to take into account that:
- all syllabus areas are equally examinable
- you need more time when revising areas of the syllabus you feel least confident about
- question practice is the best form of revision.

Make a timetable/plan to remind yourself how much
work you have to do and when you are free to do it.
Allow some time for slippage.

REVISION TECHNIQUES

- Go through your notes and study text highlighting the important points

- You might want to produce your own set of **summarised notes**

- **List key words** for each topic to remind you of the essential concepts

- **Practise exam-standard questions**, under timed conditions

- **Rework questions** that you got completely wrong the first time, but only when you think you know the subject better

- If you get stuck on topics, **find someone to explain** them to you (your tutor or a colleague, for example)

- **Read recent articles** on the ACCA website or in the student magazine

- **Read** good newspapers and professional journals

THE EXAM

FORMAT OF THE EXAM

The exam is a computer-based exam.

	Number of marks
50 multiple-choice questions (2 marks each)	100
Time allowed: 2 hours	

Answering the questions

- **Multiple-choice questions** – read the questions carefully and work through any calculations required.

- **If you don't know the answer**, eliminate those options you know are incorrect and see if the answer becomes more obvious. Remember that only one answer to a multiple choice question can be right!

- **If you get stuck with a question** skip it and return to it later.

- **Answer every question** – if you do not know the answer, you do not lose anything by guessing. Towards the end of the examination spend the last five minutes reading through your answers and making any corrections.

- **Equally divide the time** you spend on questions. In a two-hour examination that has 50 questions you have about 2.4 minutes per a question.

- **Do not skip any part of the syllabus** and make sure that you have **learnt** definitions, **know** key words and their meanings and importance, and **understand** the names and meanings of rules, concepts and theories.

- Bear in mind that this exam questions that test your understanding of narrative and computational elements, so ensure that you are able to deal with both types of question.

Computer-based examinations

- Be sure you understand how to use the **software** before you start the exam. If in doubt, ask the assessment centre staff to explain it to you.

- Questions are **displayed on the screen** and answers are entered using keyboard and mouse. At the end of the exam, you are given a certificate showing the result you have achieved.

- **Don't panic** if you realise you've answered a question incorrectly – you can always go back and change your answer.

ACCA SUPPORT

Note that from 2023–24, the detail of the syllabus for this exam has been updated. This exam kit reflects the changes to the syllabus.

For additional support with your studies please also refer to the ACCA Global website.

Section 1

STUDY SUPPORT QUESTIONS

BUSINESS TRANSACTIONS AND DOCUMENTATION

1 CASH OR CREDIT

Given below are a number of transactions. For each transaction, tick the relevant box to indicate whether it is a cash transaction or a credit transaction.

TRANSACTION		CASH	CREDIT
(a)	Receipt of goods costing $140.59 from a supplier together with an invoice for that amount.		
(b)	Payment of $278.50 by cheque for a purchase at the till.		
(c)	Receipt of a deposit of $15.00 for goods.		
(d)	Sending of an invoice for $135.00 to the payer of the deposit for the remaining value of the goods.		
(e)	Sale of goods for $14.83, payment received by credit card.		

(5 marks)

2 DOCUMENTS

Fill in the boxes to give the names of the various documents used at the following stages of the process of purchasing goods by means of cash or on credit.

(a) Request to supplier to supply goods.

(b) Notification by supplier of the amount due to be paid for the goods.

(c) Notification by purchaser to the supplier of the amount enclosed as payment.

(d) Cancellation of an amount due to a supplier.

(e) Record of a cash sale given to a customer.

(5 marks)

3 DEBIT/CREDIT NOTES

Fill in the gaps in the following sentences, which explain the difference between a debit note and a credit note.

A credit note is a document produced by the ………… and sent to the …………… which cancels all or part of ……………

A debit note, on the other hand, is raised by the ………….. and sent to the ………… requesting a …………… Not all businesses employ a formal debit note for this purpose; many rely on a letter or telephone call only. **(6 marks)**

DOUBLE ENTRY BOOKKEEPING

4 TERMINOLOGY

Fill in the gaps to identify the following terms:

(a) An …………………. is a present resource controlled by the …………… as a result of a past ……………

(b) A ………………is an amount owed by the business to another business or individual.

Examples include a ………………… and amounts owed to the suppliers of goods or services which have yet to be paid for.

(c) ………………………… is an asset comprising goods purchased for resale, components for inclusion in manufactured products, and the finished products which have been manufactured which have not yet been sold.

(d) ………………. is the liability of the business to the owner of the business.

(e) ………………… is the term which refers to amounts taken out of the business by the owner. **(10 marks)**

5 CLASSIFYING TRANSACTIONS AND BALANCES

Given below are a number of typical transactions and balances that might be found in a business.

Fill in the boxes to indicate whether the items are assets, liabilities, expenses or income.

(a) Goods stored in the warehouse awaiting resale

(b) Electricity bill paid

(c) Cash received from sale of goods

(d) Amounts owing from a customer

(e) Rent paid for the factory building

(f) Cash paid into the business by the owner

(g)   Amounts owed to suppliers

[   ]

(h)   Cash held in the till

[   ]

(i)   Machinery purchased for use in the factory

[   ]

(j)   Rent received for subletting part of the factory premises

[   ]

(k)   Cash held in the business bank account

[   ]

(11 marks)

6   BAO SMITH – ACCOUNTING EQUATION

In the following transactions the accounting equation builds up at each stage.

Use the boxes below the accounting equation to show the amounts in each category in which the transactions would be recorded and what the business owns and owes cumulatively, after each transaction.

(a)   Bao Smith starts a new business by depositing $10,000 into a business bank account.

Assets =	Capital	+ Profit	– Drawings	+ Liabilities

(b)   A bank lends the business a further $5,000.

Assets =	Capital	+ Profit	– Drawings	+ Liabilities

(c)   Bao buys a delivery van for $6,000.

Assets =	Capital	+ Profit	– Drawings	+ Liabilities

(d)   Bao buys inventory for $2,500 by writing out a business cheque.

Assets =	Capital	+ Profit	– Drawings	+ Liabilities

(e)   All of the inventory is sold for $4,000. The money is paid direct to the business bank account.

(Remember there are two elements to this transaction. Firstly, the money coming into the business and the fact that the business no longer has an inventory asset, and secondly, the calculation of profit.)

Assets =	Capital	+ Profit	– Drawings	+ Liabilities

(f)   Bao pays a business expense of $400 out of the business bank account.

Assets =	Capital	+ Profit	– Drawings	+ Liabilities

(g)   Finally Bao takes $300 out of the business for personal expenses.

Assets =	Capital	+ Profit	– Drawings	+ Liabilities

(16 marks)

7 SAMIN'S BOOKS – LEDGER ACCOUNTS

Samin begins business as a second-hand bookseller on 1 February 20X7. The transactions for the first week are listed below.

(a) Deposited $5,000 in a business bank account as the opening capital.

(b) Purchased books for $600, by paying by cheque.

(c) Sold books for $800 paid in cash.

(d) Paid rent of $500, paying by cheque.

(e) Bought a second-hand van for $2,000, paying by cheque.

Required:

For each of these transactions indicate which ledger account would be debited and which would be credited in the table given below.   **(5 marks)**

Transactions	Account to be debited	Account to be credited
(a)		
(b)		
(c)		
(d)		
(e)		

8 CHRIS FINDLAY – LEDGER ACCOUNTS

Chris Findlay opens a fishing tackle shop on 1 June 20X8. During that month Chris entered into the following transactions:

(a) Paid $1,500 into a business bank account

(b) Paid one month's rent of $230

(c) Purchased rods for $420, by cheque

(d) Purchased nets for $180, by cheque

(e) Sold some of the rods for $240 cash

(f) Purchased live bait for $10, by cheque

(g) Sold live bait for $16

(h) Purchased flies for $80, by cheque

(i) Paid shop assistant's wages of $95

(j) Sold some of the flies for $50

(k) Paid sundry expenses of $10

Required:

Record the above transactions in the following ledger accounts.   **(11 marks)**

Cash at bank account

Capital account

Rent account

Purchases account

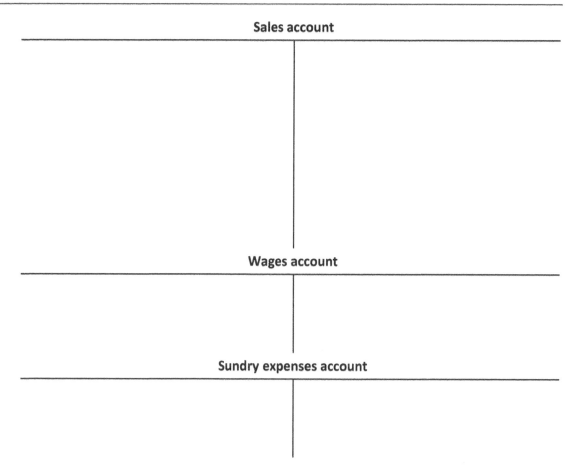

Sales account

Wages account

Sundry expenses account

9   JAY FRY – LEDGER ACCOUNTS AND BALANCING

On 14 April 20X5 Jay Fry set up a business which sold frozen fish, meat and vegetable dishes from door-to-door in a specially adapted van. The transactions for the first two weeks of trading were as follows:

(a)   Paid $10,000 of redundancy money into a business bank account

(b)   Used $3,600 to buy a second hand van by writing a cheque

(c)   Spent $1,700 by cheque having the van converted as a travelling deep freeze

(d)   Paid $400 in cash for the first consignment of frozen food

(e)   Received $110 of cheques and $80 of cash for sales in the first week of trading

(f)   Spent $260 in cash on a back-up freezer in which to store additional inventory

(g)   Paid $190 in cash for additional inventory

(h)   Received $170 of cheques and $50 of cash for sales in the second week of trading

(i)   Paid a neighbour $40 in cash as wages for help in moving inventory from the freezer to the van

(j)   Withdrew $60 in cash from the business bank account as living expenses

Required:

Fill in the boxes with the balance carried down on the following accounts:

Cash and bank account ☐

Capital account ☐

Van account ☐

Purchases account ☐

Sales account ☐

Freezer account ☐

Wages ☐

Drawings ☐

(8 marks)

Tutorial note

You may find it helpful (and useful practice) to answer this question by entering these transactions in the appropriate ledger accounts. Then calculate a balance on each ledger account.

---

10 **ASSETS OR LIABILITIES?**

Given below is a list of typical assets and liabilities that might be found in a business.

Required:

Fill in the boxes by stating whether each of the following items is either an asset or a liability.

(a) Cars for use by the sales team ☐

(b) Computers for resale ☐

(c) Bank overdraft ☐

(d) Monies owed by a customer ☐

(e) Trade payables ☐

(f) Office furniture ☐

(g) Trade receivables ☐

(7 marks)

BANKING AND PETTY CASH

11   PETTY CASH PRACTICE

On 1 August 20X4 $73.42 of cash was added to the petty cash box to top it up to the imprest amount of $200 and on 8 August a further $114.37 was put into the box in cash. Cash payments during the week ending 7 August 20X4 were evidenced by the following vouchers.

Petty Cash Voucher	No. 279

Date   1 Aug X4

For what required	AMOUNT $	¢
Tea, coffee, biscuits.	11	78

Signature   **J Small**

Authorised   **Petty cashier**

Petty Cash Voucher	No. 280

Date   1 Aug X4

For what required	AMOUNT $	¢
Taxi	3	90

Signature   **P Printer**

Authorised   **Petty cashier**

Petty Cash Voucher	No. 281

Date   2 Aug X4

For what required	AMOUNT $	¢
Window cleaner	26	00

Signature   **J Small**

Authorised   **Petty cashier**

Petty Cash Voucher	No. 282

Date   3 Aug X4

For what required	AMOUNT $	¢
Client lunch (including sales tax of $4.16)	27	90

Signature   **Rillingworth**

Authorised   **Petty cashier**

Petty Cash Voucher	No.	283		
Date 3 Aug X4				
For what required		AMOUNT	$	¢
Stamps			11	00
Signature **J Small**				
Authorised **Petty cashier**				

Petty Cash Voucher	No.	284		
Date 4 Aug X4				
For what required		AMOUNT	$	¢
Boxfiles			12	49
Paper (including sales tax of $2.90)			7	00
Signature **T Semper**				
Authorised **Petty cashier**				

Petty Cash Voucher	No.	285		
Date 4 Aug X4				
For what required		AMOUNT	$	¢
Rail fare			12	00
Signature **J Small**				
Authorised **Petty cashier**				

Petty Cash Voucher	No.	286		
Date 4 Aug X4				
For what required		AMOUNT	$	¢
Stamps			2	30
Signature **T Semper**				
Authorised **Petty cashier**				

Required:

Complete the petty cash analysis for the first week in August 20X4 by filling in the shaded boxes overleaf. **(10 marks)**

PETTY CASH ANALYSIS

Date 20X4	Receipts $	Voucher/ reference no	Details	Total payment $	Sales tax $	Office expenses $	Travel expenses $	Postage $	Stationery $	Sundry $
1 Aug	....		Balance b/d							
1 Aug	73.42		Cash from bank							
1 Aug		279	Refreshments	11 78		11 78				
1 Aug		280	Taxi	3 90			3 90			
2 Aug		281	Window cleaners	26 00		26 00				
3 Aug		282	Client lunch	......	......					......
3 Aug		283	Stamps	11 00				11 00		
4 Aug		284	Stationery	......	......				......	
4 Aug		285	Rail fare	12 00			12 00			
4 Aug		286	Stamps	2 30				2 30		
				......	......	37 78	15 90	13 30	......	......
7 Aug	200		Balance c/d	......						
				200 00						
7 Aug	....		Balance b/d							
8 Aug	....		Cash from bank							

12   IMPREST SYSTEM

Fill in the gaps in the following sentences:

Payments out of petty cash will occur when an authorised ………………………. and supporting ……………… are produced. Properly evidenced vouchers are ……………… by senior members of staff.

At the end of the month the petty cash payments will …………… the vouchers and their supporting documentation, and a cheque will be cashed at the bank for this amount so as to replenish the ………………

The vouchers etc. will be removed and …………… after having been recorded in the ……………………… The vouchers, cash and petty cash records are held securely in a box and preferably in a ……………… **(8 marks)**

13   BANKING SERVICES

Fill in the gaps in the following sentences:

Standing orders and direct debits are both methods of payment whereby the bank is instructed to pay a third party from a bank account. However, the main difference is as follows:

(i)   with a ………………… it is the payer who instructs their bank to pay a certain amount on a regular basis to the payee

(ii)   with a ……………… it is the payee that instructs the bank of the payment and specifies the amount which may alter for each payment.

Credit cards and debit cards are both methods of making payments used by consumers. However the main difference is as follows:

(i)   a ………………… is a means of purchasing goods without immediate payment. Payment is made on the total balance outstanding on the card sometime after the purchase has been made

(ii)   a ……………………… is a method of making an immediate payment for purchases but without the need to write out a cheque. On payment with a ………………… the purchaser's bank account is electronically debited immediately with the amount of the purchase. **(4 marks)**

14 PARTIES TO A CHEQUE

Consider the cheque below:

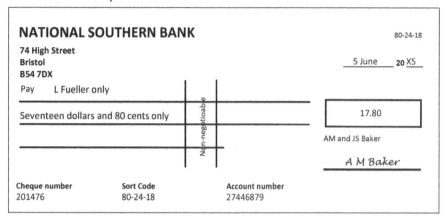

Required:

Fill in the boxes with the names of each of the following parties to the cheque:

(a)   the drawer

(b)   the drawee

(c)   the payee

(3 marks)

15 BANKING MONEY

Fill in the gaps in the following sentences:

It is important to keep cash, cheques and vouchers secure. If any are lost or stolen, this may result in financial losses to the organisation. Initially the various items tend to be kept in a …………… and any excess amount should be regularly transferred to a …….. during the day, keeping actual cash in the ……..to a minimum. Money, vouchers and so on should also be taken to the …….. regularly to reduce the amount held on premises. This could be daily, every two or three days or other intervals depending on the amount received day to day. The timing of going to the bank should be …….. so that there is not a regular pattern of visiting the bank.

…………………….. are used to include details of cash and cheques and, usually separately, card vouchers. If the business accepts a number of cheques, it is usual to supply a ……………………. which can be checked against the actual cheques by the bank to avoid or resolve problems.

If the home branch of the business is in another city, the amounts paid into the bank will need to be processed through the …………………………………….. which may take several days before it reaches the home branch. On receipt, certain items will be 'cleared' such as ………………. This amount can be used immediately. Cheques paid into the bank are subject to clearance before the amount they represent can be used as cleared funds. This period provides sufficient time for the cheques to be returned if there are any technical problems with the cheque or there are ………………………….. in the account.

If the business has a large number of staff, ……………… should be used to pay wages and salaries into the bank accounts of the staff members. This reduces the amount of cash that needs to be maintained on the premises and avoids the need to write out numerous cheques or credit transfers.

(10 marks)

16 MAINSTREAM CO – CHECKING CORRECTNESS OF REMITTANCES

You work for an organisation called Mainstream Co. In the post this morning, 12 July, the following remittance advice and cheque were received from one of your customers, Tarbick & Co.

TARBICK & CO

74 Hartston Street, Brinton, SY3 5AZ

Date: 10 July 20X5   **REMITTANCE ADVICE**

Date	Description	Amount
	Inv. 52843	361.30
	Inv. 53124	227.00
	Inv. 53128	450.20
		1,038.50
	Cheque enclosed Cheque no	1,038.50

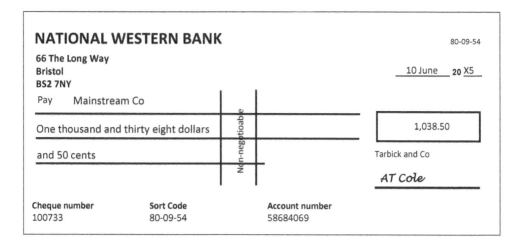

NATIONAL WESTERN BANK   80-09-54

66 The Long Way
Bristol
BS2 7NY   10 June 20 X5

Pay   Mainstream Co

One thousand and thirty eight dollars

and 50 cents   1,038.50

Non-negotioable

Tarbick and Co

AT Cole

Cheque number	Sort Code	Account number
100733	80-09-54	58684069

The receivables' ledger records for Tarbick & Co show the following position at 12 July:

Outstanding invoices

Date	Number	$
14 June	52843	316.30
27 June	53124	227.00
29 June	53128	450.20
5 July	53317	482.68

Required:

A number of errors have been made on the remittance advice. Fill in the boxes below:

(a)   The invoice number [   ] was for [   ] rather than the [   ] entered onto the remittance advice.

(b)   The revised cheque total should be [   ].   **(4 marks)**

17   YANLIN DEMPSTER – BANK LEDGER

Yanlin Dempster runs a wholesale business supplying small medical items to chemists' shops, sports clubs and local businesses. All transactions are on credit. The transactions in the first month of trading are listed below.

(a)   Opened a bank account in the name of Surgical Supplies and deposited $10,000.

(b)   Bought a delivery van for $4,000 from Vans Galore.

(c)   Sold bandages and one box of antiseptic cream to Woodside Rugby Club for $65.

(d)   Paid Vans Galore $2,000 and Surgiplast $150.

(e)   Received a cheque for $65 from Woodside Rugby Club.

(f)   Paid Yanlin Dempster's private electricity bill of $130.

Required:

(a)   Complete the following bank account.

Bank

		$			$
(a)	Capital	10,000	......	Vans Galore	....
......	Woodside Rugby Club	65	......	Surgiplast	....
			(f)	....	130
				Balance c/d	....
		———			———
		10,065			10,065
		———			———
	Balance b/d	....			

                                                                          (5 marks)

(b) **Fill in the gaps in the following sentences to explain the principles behind the treatment of transaction (f) above.**

The .... concept is the principle underlying the treatment of the owner's private expenses paid by the business. This concept requires the transactions of a .... to be recorded separately from those of the .... of a business. Consequently, this payment could not be analysed as 'electricity' as it is not the electricity expense of the business. It may be thought of as a withdrawal of cash from the business by the owner. **(5 marks)**

(Total: 10 marks)

SALES AND SALES RECORDS

18 SALES TAX

During the month of March 20X4 a business made sales on credit of $15,790 plus sales tax and purchases on credit of $12,455 inclusive of sales tax. Also during this month $13,612 was received from receivables in cash and cheques and cheque payments of $9,400 were made to payables. Sales tax is at the rate of 17.5%.

Required:

(a) **Write up these transactions by completing the following ledger accounts.** **(9 marks)**

Sales account

	$		$
Bal c/d	....	Receivables	....
	_____		_____
	....		....
	_____		_____

Receivables account

	$		$
		Cash	13,612.00
Sales	....	Bal c/d	....
	_____		_____
	....		....
	_____		_____

Purchases account

	$		$
Payables	....	Bal c/d	....
	————		————
	....		....
	————		————

Payables account

	$		$
Cash	9,400.00		
Bal c/d	....	Purchases	....
	————		————
	....		....
	————		————

Sales tax account

	$		$
Sales tax on purchases	....		
Bal c/d	....	Sales tax on sales	....
	————		————
	....		....
	————		————

(b)   **Choose the correct option to complete the following sentence:**

The balance on the sales tax account shown above represents the amount of sales tax that is **owing to/repayable by** the taxation authorities.   **(1 mark)**

(Total: 10 marks)

19   VICO LTD – POSTING SALES TRANSACTIONS

Given below is a listing of the sales invoices issued and details of cash receipts for Vico Ltd for the week ended 3 August 20X8.

Required:

You are required to write up the general ledger and receivables' ledger accounts based upon this information. (Note that you are NOT required to balance the accounts.)

(27 marks)

Sales invoice listing

Date		Invoice no.	Customer name	R/L ref	Gross	Sales tax	Net
					$	$	$
July	30	5102	Cameron Ass	045	48.18	7.17	41.01
	30	5103	AM McGee	027	159.30	23.72	135.58
	31	5104	P Rover	026	142.03	21.15	120.88
Aug	1	5105	Olivia Consultants	015	82.47	12.28	70.19
	1	5106	Montydee	003	61.48	9.15	52.33
	2	5107	Roberts Partners	007	153.20	22.81	130.39
	2	5108	A Pargeter	019	221.78	33.03	188.75
	2	5109	S Williams & Co	001	69.00	10.27	58.73
	3	5110	Owens Ltd	036	159.36	23.73	135.63
	3	5111	C Brown	035	62.70	9.33	53.37
					1,159.50	172.64	986.86

Receipts listing

Date	Narrative	Folio ref.	Bank		Sales tax		Retail sales		Receivables	
30 July	A Pargeter	019	204	30					204	30
	I Jones	009	73	20					73	20
31 July	Cameron Ass	045	37	40					37	40
	P Steven	032	116	78					116	78
1 Aug	Owens Ltd	036	217	84					217	84
2 Aug	Montydee	003	73	50					73	50
	AM McGee	027	190	54					190	54
3 Aug	Roberts Partners	007	111	62					111	62
			1,025	18					1,025	18

General ledger

Sales

	$			$
		30 July	Balance b/d	24,379.20

Receivables

	$		$
30 July Balance b/d	1,683.08		

Sales tax

	$		$
		30 July Balance b/d	352.69

Receivables ledger

S Williams & Co   **001**

	$		$
30 July Balance b/d	38.20		

Montydee   **003**

	$		$
30 July Balance b/d	73.50		

Roberts Partners   **007**

	$		$
30 July Balance b/d	279.30		

I Jones   **009**

	$		$
30 July Balance b/d	137.23		

Olivia Consultants   **015**

	$		$
30 July Balance b/d	42.61		

A Pargeter   **019**

	$		$
30 July Balance b/d	198.17		

P Rover   **026**

	$		$
30 July Balance b/d	296.38		

AM McGee   **027**

	$		$
30 July Balance b/d	335.28		

P Steven   **032**

	$		$
30 July Balance b/d	116.78		

C Brown   **035**

	$		$
30 July Balance b/d	35.10		

Owens Ltd   **036**

	$		$
30 July Balance b/d	512.74		

Cameron Associates			045
	$		$
30 July Balance b/d	335.28		

20 CREDIT LIMITS

Below are some details of credit customer account balances.

Name	Account	Credit limit	Current balance
		$	$
B T Prim	2143910Z	10,000	8,329.17
ZLT Ltd	1178947A	35,000	17,171.27
P Jones & Co	3419284A	21,000	22,457.75
A M N & Sons	4547448B	3,500	1,117.18
Claridge & Sons	7743914B	2,100	898.89
Foster Ltd	4143725A	7,500	2,379.84
Smith & Co	7143428B	1,700	1,845.45
Rowan Ltd	5671289T	12,000	8,943.71
Cozens & Sons	6143448A	21,000	18,934.21
P J Cartwright	7781821B	1,100	27.94
A Thorpe	2247981B	5,000	4,721.97

Required:

(a) **Which two customers have balances exceeding their credit limit?**   **(2 marks)**

(b) **Which three customers have credit limits in excess of $20,000?**   **(3 marks)**

(c) **Give three examples of action which can be taken to chase outstanding debts.**

(3 marks)

(Total: 8 marks)

21 LANCING CO – AGED RECEIVABLES ANALYSIS

Given below are four receivables ledger accounts for Lancing Co.

You are required to prepare an aged receivables analysis of these debts on the proforma given below. Today's date is 31 March 20X5.   **(10 marks)**

Vinehall				
	$			$
1 Jan Opening balance	127.38	15 Jan	Bank	73.57
28 Jan Invoice 22936	28.36	10 Feb	Bank	117.27
4 Feb Invoice 22975	117.27			
7 Mar Invoice 23011	72.48	31 Mar	Closing balance	154.65
	————			————
	345.49			345.49
	————			————

Cranbrook

		$			$
1 Jan	Opening balance	37.28	12 Jan	Bank	37.28
10 Jan	Invoice 22881	106.27	20 Jan	Bank	106.27
18 Jan	Invoice 22901	128.27	25 Feb	Bank	117.25
15 Feb	Invoice 22999	117.25			
6 Mar	Invoice 23008	115.36			
20 Mar	Invoice 23031	112.35	31 Mar	Closing balance	355.98
		616.78			616.78

Skinners

		$			$
1 Jan	Opening balance	227.71	7 Jan	Bank	172.36
21 Jan	Invoice 22912	103.46			
15 Feb	Invoice	71.62			
20 Feb	Invoice 23002	193.77	31 Mar	Closing balance	424.20
		596.56			596.56

Bickley

		$			$
1 Jan	Opening balance	72.36	10 Jan	Bank	51.26
15 Jan	Invoice 22941	88.20	12 Jan	Credit note C441	21.10
2 Feb	Invoice 22962	56.00	20 Feb	Bank	88.20
28 Feb	Invoice 23007	39.37	13 Mar	Bank	56.00
15 Mar	Invoice 23026	61.32	31 Mar	Closing balance	100.69
		317.25			317.25

Aged receivable listing

Customer	< 30 days	< 60 days	< 90 days	> 90 days	Total
	$	$	$	$	$
Vinehall					
Cranbrook					
Skinners					
Bickley					
Total					

PURCHASES AND PURCHASE RECORDS

22   POSTING CREDIT TRANSACTIONS

During its first month of trading a business has the following transactions:

(a)   Receipt of cash from the owner into a business bank account of $7,300

(b)   Purchases on credit of $460

(c)   Purchases for cash of $120

(d)   Payment of rent in advance of $240

(e)   Sales on credit of $330

(f)   Sales for cash of $220

(g)   Payment of wages of $90

(h)   Receipt of a loan from a friend of the owner of $2,000

(i)   Purchase on credit of furniture (a non-current asset) for $560

(j)   Receipts from accounts receivables of $330

(k)   Payments to accounts payables of $570

Required:

For each of these transactions indicate which ledger account would be debited and which would be credited in the table given below.   **(11 marks)**

Transactions	Account to be debited	Account to be credited
(a)		
(b)		
(c)		
(d)		
(e)		
(f)		
(g)		
(h)		
(i)		
(j)		
(k)		

23   SETTLEMENT DISCOUNTS

A business received a purchase invoice for the purchase of goods totalling $600 with the offer of a 3% settlement discount for early payment. The business paid early to take advantage of the early settlement discount.

The same business issued an invoice to one of its customers for $900 with a 3% settlement discount if it is paid before the normal settlement date. This customer normally takes advantage of the early settlement discount, and the sales invoice was prepared on that expectation. Subsequently, the customer paid within the required time to be eligible for the discount.

Required:

Using the following T accounts, record all the transactions above from initial invoices through to payment and dealing with the settlement discounts. **(6 marks)**

Ignore sales tax.

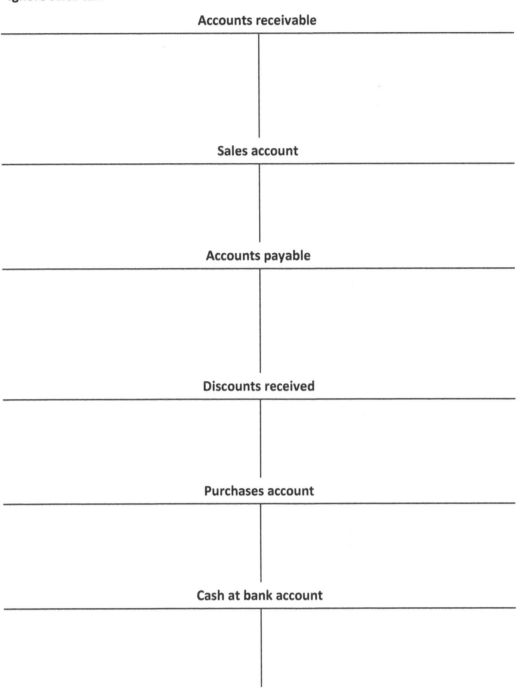

Accounts receivable

Sales account

Accounts payable

Discounts received

Purchases account

Cash at bank account

24 GEER & CO – POSTING PURCHASES TRANSACTIONS

Given below is the purchase day book and cash payments from the cash book for Geer & Co for the week ended 12 May 20X8.

You are required to write up the transactions for the week in the general ledger accounts and the payables ledger accounts of the individual suppliers.

(Note that you are NOT required to balance the accounts.) **(16 marks)**

Purchase invoice listing

Date	Invoice no.	Customer name	P/L ref.	Gross $	Sales tax $	Net $
May 8	G228	Hopkins Ltd	008	128.39	19.12	109.27
9	82456	Flute Brothers	017	48.26	7.18	41.08
9	2294	BA Johnson	012	33.71	5.02	28.69
10	29145	PGE Ltd	015	105.29	15.68	89.61
10	X8/09	Brass & Co	021	51.26	7.63	43.63
12	02268	AD Gosling	003	28.70	4.27	24.43
12	0135	Priddle & Sons	025	60.26	8.97	51.29
				455.87	67.87	388.00

Bank payments listing

Date	Cheque no.	Supplier	PL code	Total $
8 May	03362	Brass & Co	021	37.90
8 May	03363	Hopkins Ltd	008	102.64
10 May	03364	SC Basson	023	93.59
12 May	03365	Rutland Ltd	006	149.37
12 May	03366	PGE Ltd	015	93.70
				477.20

GENERAL LEDGER:

Purchases

	$		$
8 May Balance b/d	1,652.30		

Payables

	$		$
		8 May Balance b/d	912.36

Sales tax

	$		$
		8 May Balance b/d	80.41

PAYABLES LEDGER:

AD Gosling   003

	$			$
		8 May	Balance b/d	21.73

Rutland Ltd   006

	$			$
		8 May	Balance b/d	149.37

Hopkins Ltd   008

	$			$
		8 May	Balance b/d	198.37

BA Johnson   012

	$			$
		8 May	Balance b/d	–

PGE Ltd   015

	$			$
		8 May	Balance b/d	117.38

Flute Brothers   017

	$			$
		8 May	Balance b/d	88.29

Brass & Co			**021**
	$		$
		8 May Balance b/d	37.90

SC Basson			**023**
	$		$
		8 May Balance b/d	93.59

Priddle & Sons			**025**
	$		$
		8 May Balance b/d	–

25   RETURNING GOODS

Hansa received a delivery of goods and whilst unpacking them believes that they are not what was ordered. Fill in the gaps in the following sentences to explain what action should be taken to check and, if they are not what was required, how Hansa should proceed.

Hansa must check that the recollection or memory of the order is correct by referring to the ……………… This could be a copy of a ……….. order, a note of a ……………… order or an ………… confirmation of an order made over the internet. If Hansa is correct, the supplier should be ……………………….. to ensure that the correct goods are delivered and the unwanted items taken back. If there is a delay in delivering the correct goods, Hansa should ask the supplier to provide a ………………… so that there will not be a charge for the unwanted goods.

(6 marks)

PAYROLL

26 PAYROLL KNOWLEDGE

Tick the relevant box to indicate whether each of the following statements is true or false.

		TRUE	FALSE
(a)	State benefit contributions must usually be deducted from amounts paid to employees.		
(b)	All employees are entitled to a written statement of the terms and conditions of employment.		
(c)	The responsibilities of an employee are limited to what is specifically required in the contract of employment.		
(d)	State benefit contributions and income tax records may be discarded once the tax year is finished.		

(4 marks)

27 GROSS PAY – SALARIED AND PIECEWORK

Fill in the following boxes:

(a) Kadal is a monthly paid employee. On 21 June Kadal's annual salary was increased from $8,500 to $9,000. Kadal's gross pay on the pay day at the end of June was:

☐ .

(b) Lahari is paid on a piecework basis at the rate of $0.85 for every 10 units produced. In one week Lahari's production was as follows:

	Units produced
Monday	110
Tuesday	130
Wednesday	120
Thursday	140
Friday	130

Lahari's gross pay for the week is: ☐ .

(c) In the following week Lahari is told that, in addition to the basic piecework rate, there will be a bonus paid for any units produced in excess of 650 units per week. The bonus will amount to $1.05 for every 10 excess units.

Lahari's production in this week was as follows:

	Units produced
Monday	135
Tuesday	140
Wednesday	140
Thursday	150
Friday	135

Lahari's gross pay for the week was: ☐ .

(5 marks)

28   GROSS PAY – OVERTIME

Fill in the following boxes:

(a)   Paragun works a 37½-hour week for an annual salary of $14,820. Paragun is expected to work overtime of up to five hours per week without extra pay, but overtime hours in excess of this are paid at time and a half.

In one week Paragun worked 46½ hours. Paragun's gross pay for the week is

[   ]

(b)   Puran worked seven hours of overtime on top of the usual 35 hour week. Calculate Puran's overtime pay on each of the following assumptions:

(i)   Puran's normal rate of pay is $5.20 per hour and all overtime is paid at time and a half. [   ]

(ii)   Puran's normal rate of pay is $5.20 per hour and overtime is paid at the rate of time and a quarter for the first four hours overtime per week, and at time and a half thereafter. [   ]

(iii) Puran's annual salary is $10,010 and all overtime is paid at basic rate.

[   ]

(9 marks)

29   PAYSLIP

List five items which would normally appear on employee's payslip.   **(5 marks)**

30   PAYROLL ACCOUNTS

State the typical general ledger accounts which are used to account for payroll.   **(5 marks)**

BANK RECONCILIATIONS AND THE INITIAL TRIAL BALANCE

31   PHILPOTT AND SONS – SELECTING TRANSACTIONS FOR BANK RECONCILIATION

Listed below are a number of items which account for the difference between the bank statement balance and the cash at bank balance in the general ledger of Philpott and Sons on 31 October 20X8.

Tick the relevant box to show which of the following items would require adjustment in the cash at bank ledger account and which would appear as reconciling items on the bank reconciliation statement.   **(5 marks)**

ITEM		BANK LEDGER	BANK RECONCILIATION
(a)	A standing order for $230 appeared on the bank statement but had not been recorded in the bank ledger.		
(b)	A cheque for $70 written and posted to a supplier on 29 October did not appear on the bank statement until 5 November 20X8.		
(c)	A dishonoured cheque for $143 was debited on the bank statement but was not returned to Philpott and Sons until 3 November 20X8.		
(d)	The bank deducted an amount of $27 on 30 October 20X8 in respect of a standing order which had been cancelled on 1 October 20X8 in accordance with bank procedures.		
(e)	The cash and cheques banked on 31 October did not appear on the bank statement.		

32 PREPARING A BANK RECONCILIATION STATEMENT

(a) An entity's bank ledger account shows a balance of $2,369.37 on 31 May 20X4.

The bank statement recently received as at 31 May 20X4 does not include cheque payments of $394.67 and payments into the bank account totalling $936.03.

A direct debit for $393.60 appeared on the bank statement but was not entered in the bank ledger account.

The closing balance on the bank statement at 31 May is $1,434.41.

Required:

Complete the following bank ledger account and bank reconciliation statement at 31 May 20X4.   **(4 marks)**

Bank reconciliation statement at 31 May 20X4

$

Balance per bank statement   1,434.41

Less:

_____

Add:

_____

Balance per bank ledger account (working)

_____

Working:

Cash at bank

	$		$
Balance b/d	2,369.37		
	————		————
	————		————

(b) **Fill in the gaps in the following sentences which explain why bank reconciliation statements should be prepared regularly.**

The regular preparation of bank reconciliations serves as a ………. on both the organisation's records and those of the bank.

The bank reconciliation may highlight …………………. between the bank statement and the bank ledger account and these can then be …………………. and the organisation's and bank's records ………………………….

Bank reconciliations also serve as a check on the time taken to bank lodgements and for them to ……………… through the banking system.

Finally cheques that have been drawn but not yet ………………. can also be monitored in this way.

(6 marks)

(Total: 10 marks)

33 HUAN MARSHALL – LEDGER ACCOUNTS AND TRIAL BALANCE

Huan Marshall commenced trading on 5 June 20X9 by paying $6,200 into a business bank account. Huan's early transactions are as follows:

(a) Sale on credit for $441

(b) Purchase on credit for $237

(c) Payment of rent by cheque of $180

(d) Sale on credit for $118

(e) Sale for cash of $52

(f) Purchase on credit of $162

(g) Payment of wages in cash of $56

(h) Purchase for cash of $66

(i) Sale on credit of $97

(j) Payment to payables totalling $237

(k) Withdrawal of $100 in cash by the owner

(l) Receipt from receivables totalling $215

(m) Receipt of a loan of $1,000 from the bank.

Required:

Complete the following trial balance.

Note that you may find it helpful (and useful practice) to produce your workings in T-account format.

Trial balance as at...

	$	$
Cash and bank		
Capital		
Sales		
Receivables		
Purchases		
Payables		
Rent		
Wages		
Drawings		
Loan		

(Total: 28 marks)

34 ERROR CORRECTION – JOURNAL

Given below are a number of errors and omissions that have been discovered in the accounting records of an organisation.

(a) An invoice to P James for $145.79 has been entered into the individual receivables ledger account of P Jones.

(b) An invoice to H Howitt for $240 plus sales tax at 17.5% has been omitted from the accounting records.

(c) An invoice for $45.60 to M Pickering has been recorded as $54.60 in the general ledger. This invoice is for goods that are zero rated for sales tax purposes.

(d) G Fletcher owes the organisation $250 and is owed in turn $300 by the organisation. It has been agreed that these individual receivable and payable balances should be netted off against one another.

(e) $269.47 owing from J Cook is to be written off as an irrecoverable debt.

Required:

Fill in the gaps in the following journal to correct these items. **(13 marks)**

JOURNAL					
	Date		Details	Dr $	Cr $
(a)	3/3/X5		………………	145.79	
			………………..		145.79
(b)	3/3/X5		Receivables	…………	
			Sales tax		………
			Sales		………
(c)	3/3/X5		Sales	………..	
			Receivables		…….
(d)	3/3/X5		G Fletcher – …………ledger account	250.00	
			G Fletcher – …………ledger account		250.00
			……………..	250.00	
			……………..		250.00
(e)	3/3/X5		………………………..	269.47	
			………………………..		269.47

Section 2

MULTIPLE-CHOICE QUESTIONS

BUSINESS TRANSACTIONS AND DOCUMENTATION

1   Which of the following transactions is likely to occur on a daily basis in a large business organisation?

    A   Credit sales

    B   Payroll

    C   Purchase of equipment

    D   Payment of suppliers

2   Which of the following comprises small cash transactions?

    A   Payments to service providers

    B   Petty cash

    C   Purchases of inventory

    D   Receipts from sales

3   What is the purpose of a credit note?

    A   It acknowledges a purchase on credit

    B   It is a reference from an agency detailing the creditworthiness of a new customer

    C   It is issued when a deposit is paid on goods

    D   It is issued to cancel all or part of a sales invoice

4   Which of the following is NOT an internal document for purchases?

    A   Supplier list

    B   Delivery note

    C   Goods received note

    D   Purchase order

5   What is the purpose of a remittance advice?

A   To indicate items now paid

B   To identify goods received

C   To advise remittances received

D   For notification of goods dispatched

6   What is the purpose of a purchase invoice?

(i)   To claim back the sales tax

(ii)   To identify the goods bought

(iii)   To record how much is owed to the supplier

(iv)   To record how much is owed from the customer

A   (i), (ii) and (iii) only

B   All

C   (ii) and (iii) only

D   (i) and (ii) only

7   In the purchasing procedure, which document will usually follow the goods received note?

A   Delivery note

B   Invoice

C   Statement

D   Advice note

8   Salal received a document from Cullen's Stationery Supplies for eight reams of paper, which they supplied three previously. How would Salal refer to this document?

A   It is a goods received note

B   It is a receipt

C   It is a purchase invoice

D   It is a credit note

9   What is the principal document used to record petty cash transactions in the petty cash records?

A   An invoice

B   A till receipt

C   A petty cash I.O.U.

D   A petty cash voucher

10   Which of the following is a source document for financial transactions?

   A   Statement of account from a supplier

   B   Paying in slip

   C   Delivery note

   D   Goods received note

11   Which of the following is authorised so that a business can settle an outstanding invoice?

   A   A credit note

   B   A debit note

   C   A remittance advice

   D   An internal cheque requisition

12   Which of the following is an advice of employee earnings?

   A   Advice note

   B   Payslip

   C   Purchase order

   D   Quotation

13   How will a sales invoice from a supplier be regarded by its customer?

   A   As a credit note

   B   As a debit note

   C   As a purchase invoice

   D   As a receipt

14   Why must a business retain documents?

   A   Because it has always been done

   B   For historical purposes

   C   It is a requirement of tax law

   D   To facilitate planning

15   Why does data protection legislation exist?

   A   To ensure that information is maintained on employees

   B   To preserve records in business for a period of time

   C   To prevent businesses holding personal information without legitimate reason

   D   To specify the records to be maintained in respect of information technology

16 Which of the following items of personal data is excluded from the scope of typical data protection laws?

A   Data maintained regarding individual personal suppliers, such as contact details and account history

B   Data maintained regarding employees, such as employment history and contact details

C   Data maintained regarding individual personal customers, including contact details and account history

D   Personal data maintained for domestic purposes

17 Accounting systems consist of inputs, processes and outputs. Which one of the following is an input into the accounting system?

A   Employee payslips

B   The trial balance

C   Financial statements

D   Purchase invoices

18 Which one of the following is a definition of cloud accounting?

A   Cloud accounting is a computerised accounting system

B   Cloud accounting is an accounting system that enables employees to work from home

C   Cloud accounting is an accounting system that enables access to accounting software and data storage hosted on remote servers so that data and information can be accessed at any time by multiple users

D   Cloud accounting is an accounting system which can be used only by persons with a high level of computer-related knowledge

19 State whether each of the following statements is true or false.

	True/False
With a cloud accounting system, an accountant or auditor can be granted remote access to data and information they require	
With a cloud accounting system all employees are granted access to all data and information in the system	

20 What is the purpose of coding in a computerised accounting system?

A   It authorises transactions

B   It identifies appropriate accounts for posting

C   It records credit limits for accounts receivable

D   It checks ledger balances automatically

21   Kai purchased goods costing $540 plus $94.50 sales tax from Marsh Co on credit. The payables' account code is 4000, the sales tax account code is 1034 and the purchases account code is 2500.

How will this be coded and posted In Kai's computerised ledger?

A   Debit code 1034 $94.50   Credit code 2500 $540.00
     Debit code 4000 $445.50

B   Debit code 2500 $634.50   Credit code 4000 $540.00
                                                      Credit code 1034 $94.50

C   Debit code 2500 $540.00   Credit code 4000 $634.50
     Debit code 1034 $94.50

D   Debit code 4000 $634.50   Credit code 1034 $94.50
                                                      Credit code 2500 $540.00

22   Jai sold goods priced at $450 plus $78.75 sales tax from Carton Co on credit. The receivables general ledger account code is 5000, the sales tax account code is 2468 and the sales account code is 3500.

How will this be coded and posted In Jai's computerised general ledger?

A   Debit code 2468 $78.75   Credit code 3500 $528.75
     Debit code 5000 $450.00

B   Debit code 3500 $450.00   Credit code 5000 $450.00
     Debit code 2468 $78.75

C   Debit code 5000 $450.00   Credit code 3500 $528.75
     Debit code 2468 $78.75

D   Debit code 5000 $528.75   Credit code 2468 $78.75
                                                      Credit code 3500 $450.00

23   **Which one of the following is an advantage of cloud accounting?**

A   Employees of the cloud service provider can access the data of any entity it supports

B   The sharing of data and files can be done easily by multiple users

C   There is no risk of the cloud service provider suffering a cyber attack

D   There is no risk of the cloud service provider suffering a breach of security

24   **Which one of the following is a definition of cloud accounting?**

A   Cloud accounting is all computerised accounting systems and processes

B   cloud accounting is accounting hardware and software supplied by an external third party

C   Cloud accounting is accounting software that is provided by an external third party

D   Cloud accounting is access to accounting systems and processes and data storage on remote servers

25 Which one of the following is a disadvantage of cloud accounting?

A   A cloud service provider will provide services to more than one client

B   It is not possible for multiple user in multiple locations to access the services

C   All clients of the cloud service provider are reliant upon the financial stability of the service provider to continue to provide services

D   The cloud service provider does not need to comply with data protection regulations

26 Which one of the following is definition of a faceted or hierarchical coding system?

A   It is a code based upon the random generation and selection of numbers

B   The codes are broken down into a number of fields, with each field signifying a unit of information

C   It is a code based solely upon numbers

D   It is code organised in sequential order

27 Which one of the following is a definition of a mnemonic coding system?

A   It is a coding system based solely upon numbers

B   It is a coding system based solely upon letters of the alphabet

C   It is a coding system based upon the generation of random codes using both number and letters of the alphabet

D   It is a coding system based upon the use of both numbers and letters of the alphabet

28 A computerised accounting system produces a statement of account for each credit customer, which is then issued to each customer as a reminder to pay amounts due.

Which one of the following is an advantage of this system?

A   The statements are produced independently from the sales system

B   All amounts due will be received from customers

C   Each statement is based upon data recorded in the general ledger

D   None of the statements will contain errors or omissions

29 The employees of Manx Co use a personal smart fob to record the time they arrive and leave work each day. This information is then used by the automated wages system to produce the monthly payroll totals and payslips.

Which one of the following is an advantage of this system?

A   The processing of payroll information and payslips is more efficient and reliable than a manual system

B   An employee will never forget to use their personal smart fob

C   Supervisors no longer need to review and approve working hours for each employee

D   It is not possible for there to be any errors in the payroll totals and payslips produced

30 Coypu Co is an online video games retailer and operates a computerised accounting system, which includes integrated sales and inventory systems. It maintains an inventory of over 5,000 items, across an extensive range of video games.

Which one of the following is not an advantage of a computerised accounting system?

A   Sales to individual customers are straightforward to record

B   It is easy to trace and track orders for new games from individual customers

C   The inventory system can be interrogated quickly and easily to confirm the inventory level of any game at any time

D   Computerised accounting records are never wrong

31 Llama Co is registered to account for sales tax and operates a computerised accounting system. Llama Co is producing training materials for its newly recruited staff relating to data inputs for the purchasing system.

Which one of the following is not an item of standing data used by the purchasing system to process invoices, credit notes and payments?

A   The bank account details of each supplier to enable automated payments to be made when due

B   The credit terms agreed with each supplier

C   The rate of sales tax applicable when the supplier is registered to account for sales tax

D   A purchase invoice

32 Camel Co operates a computerised accounting system. Llama Co is producing training materials for its newly recruited staff relating to data inputs for the sales system.

Which one of the following is not a source document used to update the sales system to process invoices, credit notes and receipts from customers?

A   A credit note issued to a customer

B   The credit terms agreed with each customer

C   A detailed listing of bank receipts from customers

D   A sale invoice

DUALITY OF TRANSACTIONS AND THE DOUBLE-ENTRY SYSTEM

33 Taaj started a business by paying $5,000 into a business bank account.

What are the accounting entries required to record this?

A	Dr	Capital $5,000	Cr	Bank $5,000
B	Dr	Bank $5,000	Cr	Capital $5,000
C	Dr	Bank $5,000	Cr	Drawings $5,000
D	Dr	Drawings $5,000	Cr	Bank $5,000

34 Ade started a taxi business by transferring a car, valued at $5,000, into the business.

What are the accounting entries required to record this?

A	Dr	Capital $5,000	Cr	Car $5,000
B	Dr	Car $5,000	Cr	Drawings $5,000
C	Dr	Car $5,000	Cr	Capital $5,000
D	Dr	Car $5,000	Cr	Bank $5,000

35 Jones' account is shown below:

Jones

		$			$
1 January	Bal b/d	250	17 January	Returns out	50
12 January	Sales	1,000	28 January	Bank	800
23 January	Sales	500	31 January	Bal c/d	900
		1,750			1,750
1 February	Bal b/d	900			

What is the balance on Jones' account as at 31 January?

A   Debit $250

B   Debit $1,750

C   Debit $900

D   Credit $900

36 Which of the following changes could NOT occur as a result of an entry in the bookkeeping records?

A   Increase asset and increase liability

B   Increase asset and increase capital

C   Increase capital and increase liability

D   Increase capital and decrease liability

37 A business has capital of $10,000 and liabilities of $4,000.

Which of the following asset and liability figures could appear in this business' statement of financial position?

A	Assets	$6,000	Liabilities	$16,000
B	Assets	$6,000	Liabilities	$4,000
C	Assets	$10,000	Liabilities	$10,000
D	Assets	$14,000	Liabilities	$4,000

38   What is the double entry to record receipt of cash from an account receivable?

A   Debit sales   Credit receivables

B   Debit receivables   Credit cash at bank

C   Debit cash at bank   Credit sales

D   Debit cash at bank   Credit receivables

39   A sole trader had opening capital of $10,000 and closing capital of $4,500. During the accounting period, the owner introduced capital of $4,000 and withdrew $8,000 for own use.

What was the profit or loss for the accounting period?

A $9,500 loss

B $1,500 loss

C $7,500 profit

D $17,500 profit

40   What does a debit balance usually represent?

A   Assets and income

B   Liabilities and income

C   Assets and expenses

D   Liabilities and expenses

41   What is the double entry required to record the purchase of a motor van on credit?

A   Debit: motor expenses   Credit: cash at bank

B   Debit: motor van   Credit: cash at bank

C   Debit: motor expenses   Credit: payables

D   Debit: motor van   Credit: payables

42   What is the double entry required to record the withdrawal of cash from a business bank account by the owner?

A   Debit: drawings   Credit: cash at bank

B   Debit: drawings   Credit: capital

C   Debit: liability   Credit: cash at bank

D   Debit: capital   Credit: drawings

43   What is the usual double entry to record the sale of inventory for cash?

A   Debit: inventory account   Credit: sales account

B   Debit: cash account   Credit: sales account

C   Debit: cash account   Credit: inventory account

D   Debit: cash account   Credit: inventory account

44 A debit balance would be expected to arise when the accounts are balanced at the period end on which of the following accounts?

A Capital

B Sales

C Electricity

D Loan

45 A credit balance would be expected to arise when the accounts are balanced at the period end on which of the following accounts?

A Drawings

B Telephone

C Receivables

D Payables

46 A business sells goods on credit to a customer who pays one month later. What are the accounting entries required to record the receipt of cash from the customer?

A Debit: Cash at bank account   Credit: Receivables

B Debit: Cash at bank account   Credit: Payables

C Debit: Receivables   Credit: Cash at bank account

D Debit: Payables   Credit: Cash at bank account

47 Which of the following describes the separate entity principle?

A The assets of a business are a separate entity from the liabilities

B The drawings of a business are a separate entity from the profit of the business

C The business is a separate entity from the owner of the business

D The owner of the business must be a separate entity from a lender to the business

48 Which of the following is a liability?

A Trade receivables

B Inventory

C Bank overdraft

D Drawings

49 Which of the following is NOT an asset?

A Owner's capital

B Petty cash

C Salesman's motor car

D Computer software

50 Which of the following statements describes the accounting equation?

A   Net assets = Capital – Profit – Drawings

B   Net assets = Capital – Profit + Drawings

C   Net assets = Capital + Profit + Drawings

D   Net assets = Capital + Profit – Drawings

51 When goods are taken out of the business for personal use by the owner of a business, how will they be recorded?

A   As drawings

B   As an expense

C   As inventory

D   As a liability

52 If the owner of a business withdraws cash from the business bank account in order to meet personal expenses, this is classified as drawings.

What is this an example of?

A   Internal control

B   Personal ledger accounting

C   Segregation of duties

D   The separate entity principle

53 What is the effect upon net assets when inventory is purchased on credit?

A   Net assets and owner's capital do not change

B   Net assets increase and owner's capital increase

C   Net assets decrease and owner's capital decreases

D   Net assets increase and owner's capital stays the same

54 What is the effect upon net assets when an expense is paid in cash?

A   Net assets increase and profit increases

B   Net assets decrease and profit decreases

C   Net assets remain the same and profit increases

D   Net assets remain the same and profit decreases

55 What is the general ledger?

A   It is a record of all transactions before being posted to ledger accounts.

B   It is a record which contains a ledger account for each type of asset, liability, expense and income.

C   It is a record which contains all of the details of the non-current assets.

D   It is a record which contains all of the details of individual receivable accounts.

56   **What is a ledger account?**

A   It is a record of all transactions relating to all asset and liability accounts.

B   It is a record of all transactions relating to an individual credit customer.

C   It is a record of all transactions that have passed through the bank account.

D   It is a record of transactions assigned to a specific item, such as an expense, an asset, a liability an item of income or capital.

57   **What is the payables ledger?**

A   A record of the credit limits of each credit supplier

B   A record of the personal details of each credit supplier

C   A record of the accounts of each credit supplier

D   A record of the accounts of each credit customer

58   **Which of the following would normally be a debit balance on a general ledger account?**

(i)   Sales revenues (sales)

(ii)   Rent

(iii)   Drawings

(iv)   Capital

A   (i) and (iii)

B   (ii) and (iii)

C   (i) and (iv)

D   (ii) and (iv)

59   **Which of the following statements is true?**

A   Purchase of a salesman's car is asset expenditure and repairs to a delivery van are expenses.

B   Repairs to a delivery van are asset expenditure and rent for a factory is an expense.

C   Purchase of a salesman's car is asset expenditure and purchase of computers for office use is an expense.

D   Purchase of shelving for the office is asset expenditure and purchase of computers for office use is an expense.

60 **Which of the following are examples of asset expenditure?**

(i)   Purchase of a new computer for office use

(ii)   Purchase of a second hand computer for office use

(iii)   Repairs to the computer

(iv)   Purchase of additional hardware to enhance the computer

A   (i) only

B   (i) and (iv)

C   (i), (ii) and (iv)

D   All four

61 **Which of the following is an example of an expense?**

(i)   Purchase of a second hand delivery van

(ii)   Purchase of inventories for resale

(iii)   Repairs to the delivery van

(iv)   Insurance of the delivery van

A   (i), (ii) and (iii)

B   (i), (ii) and (iv)

C   (ii), (iii) and (iv)

D   (iii) and (iv)

62 **Which of the following types of expenditure would be classified as asset expenditure?**

A   Legal fees associated with the purchase of an office

B   Repairs to a delivery van

C   Rent of a leasehold property for five years

D   Repainting the office premises

63 **Which of the following types of expenditure would be classified as an expense?**

A   Payment of tax

B   Purchase of a delivery van by a courier service

C   Extension to the office building of a toy manufacturer

D   Swivel chairs for resale by an office equipment retailer

64 **Which of the following is an asset?**

A   Bank deposit account

B   Bank overdraft

C   Bank loan

D   Proprietors' capital

65 **Which of the following is NOT an item of asset expenditure?**

A   Capital

B   Purchase of a new motor van

C   Purchase of a second hand factory machine

D   Replacement of the managing director's Mercedes car

66 A machinery account has a debit balance of $4,000.

What balances will occur at the end of the year to take this balance into the next period?

A   Dr Machinery balance c/d   Cr Machinery balance b/d

B   Cr Machinery balance c/d   Dr Machinery balance b/d

C   Dr Machinery balance c/d   Dr Machinery balance b/d

D   Cr Machinery balance c/d   Cr Machinery balance b/d

67 A capital account has a credit balance of $40,000.

What balances will occur at the end of the year to take this balance into the next period?

A   Dr Capital balance c/d   Cr Capital balance b/d

B   Cr Capital balance c/d   Dr Capital balance b/d

C   Dr Capital balance c/d   Dr Capital balance b/d

D   Cr Capital balance c/d   Cr Capital balance b/d

68 A business has a bank overdraft of $350 and $50 cash at the end of the accounting period.

What balances will be brought down at the start of the next accounting period?

A   Dr Bank   Cr Cash

B   Cr Bank   Dr Cash

C   Dr Bank   Dr Cash

D   Cr Bank   Cr Cash

69 A business purchased equipment costing $1,000 for use in the business and disposed of some old equipment during the year at a cost of $800 when purchased several years earlier. The opening balance of the equipment account was $1,000.

What will be the balance carried down to the next accounting period?

A   Dr $800

B   Cr $800

C   Dr $1,200

D   Cr $1,200

70 A business purchased machinery costing $2,000 and sold some old machinery which had cost $1,800. The opening balance of the equipment account was $2,000.

What will be the balance brought down in the next accounting period?

A   Dr $1,800

B   Cr $1,800

C   Dr $2,200

D   Cr $2,200

71 A sole trader had opening capital of $20,000 and closing capital of $23,000. During the period, the owner introduced capital of $4,000 and withdrew $15,000 for own use.

What was the sole trader's profit or loss during the accounting period?

A $8,000 profit

B $14,000 profit

C $15,000 profit

D $22,000 profit

72 **What does a credit entry usually represent?**

A   An increase in assets or income

B   An increase in liabilities or income

C   An increase in assets or expenses

D   An increase on liabilities or expenses

73 **What is the double entry to record the purchase of plant and machinery for by automated bank payment?**

A   Debit: plant repairs   Credit: cash at bank

B   Debit: plant and machinery   Credit: cash at bank

C   Debit: plant repairs   Credit: payables

D   Debit: plant and machinery   Credit: payables

74 **What is the double entry to record the introduction of capital into the business by the owner?**

A   Debit: drawings   Credit: cash at bank

B   Debit: cash at bank   Credit: drawings

C   Debit: cash at bank   Credit: capital

D   Debit: capital   Credit: cash at bank

75 A business purchased goods on credit from a supplier and will pay one month later. When the payment is made, what is the double entry required to record this?

A   Debit: Cash at bank   Credit: Receivables

B   Debit: Cash at bank   Credit: Payables

C   Debit: Receivables   Credit: Cash at bank

D   Debit: Payables   Credit: Cash at bank account

76 Which one of the following is a liability?

A   Capital introduced

B   Inventory

C   Bank overdraft

D   Drawings

77 Which one of the following is NOT an asset?

A   Computer equipment

B   Petty cash balance

C   Office photocopier

D   Computer maintenance

78 Which of the following items are examples of asset expenditure?

(i)   Purchase of a new company car for a member of staff

(ii)   Purchase of a second-hand company car for a member of staff

(iii) Repairs to company cars

(iv)   Cost of insuring company cars

A   (i) only

B   (i) and (ii)

C   (i), (ii) and (iv)

D   All four items are asset expenditure

79   Which of the following items are examples of an expense?

(i)   Purchase of a colour printer for the office

(ii)   Purchase of paper for use in the printer

(iii)   Repairs to the printer

(iv)   Purchase of ink cartridges for the printer

A   (i), (ii) and (iii)

B   (i), (ii) and (iv)

C   (ii), (iii) and (iv)

D   (iii) and (iv)

80   Which of the following examples of expenditure should be classified as asset expenditure?

A   Painting and decoration of the office

B   Purchase of a delivery van

C   Capital introduced

D   Drawings

81   Which of the following items correctly represents the accounting equation?

A   Assets = liabilities

B   Assets = Liabilities – proprietor's capital

C   Assets = proprietor's capital

D   Assets = Proprietor's capital + liabilities

82   Which of the following statements best explains the accounting equation?

A   The accounting equation demonstrates the effect of a transaction upon the assets, liabilities and proprietor's capital of a business.

B   The accounting equation demonstrates the impact a transaction on the statement of profit or loss for the year.

C   The accounting equation demonstrates the effect of a transaction upon the assets and income of a business.

D   The accounting equation demonstrates the effect of a transaction upon the expenses and liabilities of a business.

83   Which of the following statements illustrates the accounting equation?

A   Closing net assets = Opening capital – Profit – Drawings

B   Closing net assets = Opening capital – Profit + Drawings

C   Closing net assets = Opening capital + Profit + Drawings

D   Closing net assets = Opening capital + Profit – Drawings

84	**Which of the following statements provides a definition of an asset?**

A	It is a present obligation of the entity to transfer an economic resource as a result of past events

B	It is a present economic resource controlled by the entity as a result of past events

C	It is the excess of revenue over expenses for a period of time

D	It is the net investment in the business by the proprietor

85	**Which of the following statements provides a definition of a liability?**

A	It is a present obligation of the entity to transfer an economic resource as a result of past events

B	It is a present economic resource controlled by the entity as a result of past events

C	It is the excess of revenue over expenses for a period of time

D	It is a decrease or outflow of economic benefits resulting from a transaction

86	**Which of the following statements provides a definition of capital?**

A	It is the accumulated profit in the business due to the proprietor

B	It is the capital introduced into the business by the proprietor

C	It is the net investment in the business by the proprietor

D	It is the accumulated profits less accumulated losses made by the business

87	**Which of the following transactions would have no impact upon total assets within the accounting equation?**

A	The injection of cash into the business by the owner

B	A receipt from a credit customer paying the amount due

C	The settlement of an outstanding payables to a credit supplier

D	The purchase of a machine on credit

88	**What is the purpose of a ledger account?**

A	It enables a business to classify record and summarise transactions in an orderly and consistent manner

B	It enables a business to identify the value of assets and liabilities at any point in time

C	It enables a business to determine whether a business made a profit or a loss during an accounting period

D	It enables a business to determine the capital account balance of the proprietor at any point in time

89 **Which of the following statements best describes current assets?**

A   Assets which are currently located on the business premises

B   Assets which are used to conduct the organisation's current business

C   Assets which are expected to be converted into cash in the short term

D   Assets which are not expected to be converted into cash in the short term

90 **Which of the following statements best describes non-current assets?**

A   Assets which are used in the business over a number of accounting periods to undertake the activities of the organisation.

B   Assets which are used to conduct the organisation's current business.

C   Assets which are expected to be converted into cash in the short term.

D   Assets which can be used to convert into cash in the short-term or to be used in the business over a number of accounting periods.

91 **Which of the following statements best describes non-current liabilities?**

A   Liabilities which have not yet been incurred, but which will be incurred with the next twelve months.

B   Liabilities which will only be paid upon termination of a business.

C   Liabilities which will fall due for payment within twelve months of the reporting date.

D   Liabilities which will fall due for payment after more than twelve months from the reporting date.

92 **Which of the following statements best describes a current liability?**

A   It is a liability which has not yet been incurred, but which will be incurred with the next twelve months.

B   It is a liability which will only be paid upon termination of a business.

C   It is a liability which will fall due for payment within twelve months of the reporting date.

D   It is a liability which will fall due for payment after more than twelve months from the reporting date.

93 **Which of the following statements provides a definition of an asset?**

A   It is a present obligation of the entity to transfer an economic resource as a result of past events

B   It is a present economic resource controlled by the entity as a result of past events

C   It is the excess of revenue over expenses for a period of time

D   It is the net investment in the business by the proprietor

94 **Which of the following statements provides a definition of a liability?**

A   It is a present obligation of the entity to transfer an economic resource as a result of past events

B   It is a present economic resource controlled by the entity as a result of past events

C   It is the excess of revenue over expenses for a period of time

D   It is a decrease or outflow of economic benefits resulting from a transaction

95 **Which of the following statements provides a definition of capital?**

A   It is the accumulated profit in the business due to the proprietor

B   It is the capital introduced into the business by the proprietor

C   It is the net investment in the business by the proprietor

D   It is the accumulated profits less accumulated losses made by the business

96 **Which elements of the financial statements are summarised and classified in the statement of financial position?**

A   Assets and liabilities

B   Assets, liabilities and capital

C   Income and expenses

D   Income, expenses and capital

97 **Which elements of the financial statements are summarised and classified in the statement of profit or loss?**

A   Income, expenses and capital

B   Income and expenses

C   Assets and liabilities

D   Assets, liabilities and capital

98 **Which statement provides the definition of a statement of profit or loss?**

A   A statement that presents a summary of the assets, liabilities and capital of a business at a specific date

B   A statement that presents a summary of the assets and liabilities of a business at a specific date

C   A statement that presents a summary of the income and expenses of a business for a period of time

D   A statement that presents a summary of the assets and liabilities of a business for a period of time

99 Which statement provides the definition of a statement of financial position?

A   A statement that presents a summary of the income and expenses of a business for a period of time

B   A statement that presents a summary of the assets and liabilities of a business at a specific date

C   A statement that presents a summary of the assets and liabilities of a business for a period of time

D   A statement that presents a summary of the assets, liabilities and capital of a business at a specific date

100 Which **TWO** of the following items are a component of a set of financial statements produced by a sole trader?

	Selected answer
Statement of financial position	
Bank statement	
Statement of profit or loss	
Supplier statement	

BANK SYSTEM AND TRANSACTIONS

101 Which of the following is the most efficient method of filing and retaining purchase invoices received from suppliers?

A   Supplier name only in alphabetical order

B   Purchase invoice date only

C   Using both supplier name in alphabetical order and purchase invoice date

D   Supplier purchase invoice number only

102 What are the disadvantages of an organisation not having a document retention policy?

(i)   Difficulty trying to demonstrate compliance with any legal or regulatory requirements relating to business documents.

(ii)   Difficulty and wasted time trying to locate and access individual documents.

(iii)   Difficulty for an organisation to raise queries with customers and/or suppliers if a discrepancy is identified.

(iv)   Difficulty for an organisation to resolve queries raised by customers and/or suppliers.

A   All of the above

B   (i), (ii) and (iii) only

C   (ii) and (iii) only

D   (i), (ii) and (iv) only

103 **Which of the following is the most efficient method of filing and retaining sales invoices?**

A Calendar month order only

B Sequential sales invoice number order only

C Customer name only in alphabetical order

D Product reference number of items sold only

104 **Why should an organisation retain completed purchase requisitions?**

A It confirms the value of a sale to a customer by an organisation

B It is confirmation that the goods in question were received

C It contains evidence of authorisation by a responsible person to confirm that there is a valid requirement or the goods/services requested

D It is confirmation that payment was made for the goods in question

105 **What are the advantages of an organisation having a document retention policy?**

(i) It enables an organisation to more easily locate and access documents.

(ii) It enables an organisation to review transactions and resolve queries raised by customers and/or suppliers.

(iii) It enables an organisation to review transactions and to raise queries with customers and/or suppliers if a discrepancy is identified.

(iv) It enables an organisation to meet any legal or regulatory requirements relating to retention of business documents.

A (i), (ii) and (iv) only

B (ii) and (iii) only

C (i), (ii) and (iii) only

D All of the above

106 Kanaka had a bank overdraft of $500 at 1 January. Kanaka's only transactions during that month were the sale of goods for cash of $900 and the purchase of goods on credit for $700.

At 31 January, what will be the balance on Kanaka's cash at bank account?

A $300 credit

B $400 debit

C $700 debit

D $1,400 debit

107 Which of the following transactions would NOT be classified as a cash transaction?

A Purchase of raw materials at a cost of $850, paid by cheque at the time of purchase.

B Sale of four chairs to Mr Jones who will pay by cheque next week.

C A transfer from the bank deposit account to the bank current account.

D Takings placed in the shop till throughout the day.

108 Which of the following could NOT be used as a method of payment?

A Credit card

B Banker's draft

C Standing order

D Remittance advice

109 What is the title of the person who signs a cheque to authorise payment?

A The drawer

B The drawee

C The payer

D The payee

110 If a cheque has been signed by the payee on the reverse side, together with a written instruction to pay a third party, what is this known as:

A An endorsement

B A cheque guarantee

C A crossed cheque

D A credit transfer

111 An individual has a card issued by the bank that enables purchases up to a certain credit limit to be made. The individual receives a statement each month detailing the purchases made and the individual is required to pay off the total amount of the balance outstanding each month.

What is this an example of?

A A debit card

B A credit card

C A charge card

D A cheque guarantee card

112 Each month the amount of money that you owe on a store credit card is paid automatically and directly to the store out of your bank account. The amount and the precise date of payment will vary each month.

What is this an example of?

A   A standing order

B   A credit transfer

C   A mail transfer

D   A direct debit

113   Who is the drawee of a cheque?

A   The person or business who is paying

B   The person or business who is being paid

C   The person who signs the cheque

D   The bank of the person or business who is paying

114   If two parallel vertical lines are drawn on the face of a cheque, what does this mean?

A   Only the payee can cash the cheque at the bank.

B   This cheque can only be deposited in the payee's bank account.

C   This cheque cannot be cashed at the bank, it can only be paid into a bank account.

D   This is now a bearer cheque which is payable to the holder.

115 There is a card which can be used to pay for goods, the amount of which is electronically deducted from your bank balance immediately.

What type of card is this?

A   A debit card

B   A credit card

C   A cheque guarantee card

D   A charge card

116 Goldie makes regular quarterly payments for gas and electricity. Goldie completed a form of authorisation and the suppliers then set up their own arrangement with the bank to collect amounts due. Goldie is always informed of these amounts in advance.

What is this method of payment?

A   A direct debit

B   An inter-bank transfer

C   A standing order

D   EFTPOS

117 What is the title of a note that accompanies a cheque payment to a supplier, detailing the invoices being paid?

    A   A supplier's statement

    B   A debit note

    C   A remittance advice

    D   A remittance list

118 Kavala pays a monthly bill for heat and light charges by instructing the bank to make a monthly payment from the business bank account in favour of the power supply company. As Kavala's power usage will change each month, Kavala's authorisation to the bank does not require the issue a new instruction to the bank to pay the revised amount to the power company.

    Which method of payment is Kavala using?

    A   Crossed cheque

    B   Direct debit

    C   Standing order

    D   Payable order

119 Who is the drawer of a cheque?

    A   The recipient of the cheque who has received the cheque as a form of payment

    B   The account holder whose account will be debited when the cheque is presented

    C   The bank and branch upon which the cheque is drawn

    D   The bank and branch through which the cheque is presented for payment

120 What card will normally be requested to accompany a payment by cheque?

    A   Credit card

    B   Cheque guarantee card

    C   Mastercard

    D   Store card

121 What information/details on a credit card should a cashier check when they receive a payment for goods?

    (i)   It is signed

    (ii)   It is valid at that day's date

    (iii)   It has not been altered/tampered with

    (iv)   It is issued by a bank

    A   All

    B   (i), (ii) and (iii) only

    C   (i) and (ii) only

    D   (ii) and (iv) only

122 What is the normal period of time required for a cheque to be cleared between banks using the UK clearing system?

A   7 working days

B   5 working days

C   10 working days

D   3 working days

123 Which of the following constitute a contractual relationship between a bank and its customers?

(i)   Receivable/Payable

(ii)   Principal/Agent

(iii) Mortgagor/Mortgagee

(iv)   Bailor/Bailee

A   All

B   (i) and (iv) only

C   (i) and (ii) only

D   (i), (ii) and (iii) only

124 A petty cash system operates on a $120 imprest system. At the end of a month there is $67.23 of valid petty cash vouchers in the petty cash box. How much cash should be taken out of the bank account in order to restore it to the correct amount?

A $52.77

B $67.23

C $120.00

D $187.23

125 Which of the following are duties of the customer towards their bank?

(i)   Promote the bank's services

(ii)   Not encourage fraudulent activities

(iii) Not to misuse any cheque guarantee card

(iv)   Not to open an account elsewhere without notice

A   All

B   (i), (ii) and (iv) only

C   (ii) and (iii) only

D   (i), (ii) and (iii) only

126 On a particular day, the cash register in a shop shows that cash sales were made of $1,073.21. The cash in the till at the end of the day totalled $1,318.76 and a cash float of $250 is always carried in the till.

Which of the following would NOT be a valid reason for the difference between the cash in the till and the cash register records?

A   All of the cash received was not paid into the till

B   A customer was given too much change

C   The price for goods entered into the cash register was higher than that charged to the customer

D   The price for goods entered into the cash register was lower than that charged to the customer

127 **What should happen to a cheque on which F Jones is the drawer and A Smith is the payee and which also contains the crossing "Account payee"?**

A   It can be paid out in cash when presented at the bank

B   It must be paid into a bank account, although there is no restriction on which bank account it is paid into

C   It must be paid into a bank account in the name of A Smith

D   It must be paid into a bank account in the name of F Jones

128 A cash advance of $20 is taken out of the petty cash box by an employee for refreshments for a client and an authorised voucher for $20 put into the petty cash box. The employee only spends $17.65 on refreshments.

What is the petty cash procedure required?

A   The employee keeps the change of $2.35

B   The employee keeps the change of $2.35 and the petty cash voucher is altered to read $17.65

C   The employee returns the $2.35

D   The employee returns the $2.35 and the petty cash voucher is altered to read $17.65

129 A member of the accounts department was permitted by a colleague to take $25 from petty cash for personal use having agreed to repay the amount later in the week.

How should this be recorded?

A   The payment must be reimbursed from the employee's salary at the end of the month

B   The payment should be recorded on a petty cash voucher immediately

C   The payment need not be recorded as the employee has agreed to repay the amount taken by the end of the week

D   The payment need only be recorded if the employee does not repay the amount due by the end of the week

130 Acme Co operates a petty cash imprest system with an imprest amount of $100, with the petty cash account reconciled and the imprest amount restored at the end of each month. During the month of April, there were petty cash payments of $17.23, $13.84, $7.62 and $23.43. Also during that month, the office drinks machine was emptied and coins totalling $53.50 were added to the float and recorded.

What is the petty cash procedure required at 30 April?

A The imprest amount is restored by making a withdrawal from the bank account of $62.12

B The imprest amount is restored by making a withdrawal from the bank account of $37.88

C The imprest amount is restored by making a withdrawal from the bank account of $8.62

D The imprest amount is restored by making a withdrawal from the bank account of $46.50

131 A Nail Co operates a petty cash imprest system, with a maximum float of $75. At 31 July, the cash in the petty cash float totalled $27.18 and the vouchers for petty cash payments made during the month were $8.63, $15.58 and $8.61 respectively. It was discovered that, shortly before the reconciliation was performed, that a payment of $15 from petty cash had been made but not recorded.

What was the amount of the reimbursement required to restore the imprest amount at 31 July?

A $60.00

B $32.82

C $47.82

D $42.18

132 Which of the following documents would be required when paying in the daily takings to the bank?

(i) Cheques received

(ii) Copy credit card vouchers

(iii) Cheque remittance list

(iv) Copy credit card summary

A (i) and (ii) only

B (i), (ii) and (iv) only

C (i), (iii) and (iv) only

D All four

133 A petty cash system is operated on an imprest system of $100. At 31 March the cash in the petty cash box totalled $36.58 and the vouchers totalled $53.42.

Which of the following would NOT be a valid reason for the difference?

A Money had been taken out of the petty cash box without an authorised voucher to support it.

B The incorrect amount of cash had been paid out of the petty cash box in for an authorised voucher.

C A petty cash voucher had been made out for the wrong amount but the amount of cash paid out agreed with the voucher.

D A petty cash voucher had been made out for the wrong amount but the correct amount of cash had been paid out.

134 Lochan is preparing a bank paying-in slip at the end of the working day. The till roll shows sales of $193.24. Lochan always maintains a float of $25 in the till and takes $20 each day for personal use.

How much will Lochan pay into the bank today?

A $213.24

B $193.24

C $173.24

D $148.24

135 **For which of the following payments would petty cash NOT normally be used?**

A $9.50 for cleaning the shop windows

B $26.00 for coffee and tea for office staff

C $525.00 invoice for transport and delivery services provided by a courier

D $37.00 train fare to a business conference

136 At 1 March, the petty cash tin contained a float of $65. During that month, petty cash payments totalled $64 and a cheque for $50 was cashed at the bank to replenish the float.

What was the petty cash float at 31 March?

A $1

B $51

C $75

D $80

137 **Where should the petty cash float be kept?**

A In a drawer

B On the desk

C In a safe

D On a cabinet

138   What is the purpose of petty cash?

A   To act as a cash float

B   To cover all out of pocket expenses

C   To pay small and/or irregular amounts

D   To finance the office parties

139   How can you ensure that petty cash payments have been made for authentic expenditure?

A   By recording the vouchers immediately in the petty cash records

B   By ensuring the petty cash vouchers are signed

C   By stapling appropriate receipts to the vouchers

D   Allowing only authorised employees to have access to petty cash

140   In January a business receives a cheque dated January of the previous year. What should it do with this cheque?

A   Pay it into the bank

B   Alter the date

C   Write 'refer to drawer' on the cheque

D   Return it to the customer for alteration or the issue of a replacement

141   Which form of payment commonly uses BACS?

A   Cheque

B   Credit card

C   Debit card

D   Payroll

142   What information is disclosed on a bank statement?

A   The transactions passing through the bank account of a business

B   The transactions between customer and supplier

C   Petty cash transactions

D   Transactions on a company credit card

143   When presenting a debit card to pay for goods at a supermarket checkout, the card is rejected with the message that the limit has been exceeded.

What action should the checkout operator take?

A   Ask the customer to make payment by some other means

B   Authorise an increased debit card limit for the customer

C   Call the police and have the customer arrested

D   Let the customer take the goods and come back later to make payment

144 **Which of the following is a valid method of payment?**

A   A credit card in excess of its limit

B   A cheque on which the amounts in words and figures differ

C   Cash

D   Barter

145 **What is needed for a cheque to be properly authorised?**

A   Sufficient money in the bank

B   Evidence of an underlying transaction and an approved requisition

C   A receipt stapled to an invoice

D   A remittance advice and the accompanying statement from supplier

146 **A cheque is automatically printed by a computerised accounting system for payment to be made to the supplier. How does this benefit the business?**

A   It prevents fraud

B   There are unlikely to be technical mistakes on the cheque

C   The cheque does not require authorisation

D   It saves the need to check and sign the cheque

147 **Why should tills be checked from time to time by managers and other responsible staff who are NOT usually involved in the receipt and payment of cash?**

A   To enable the managers and others to handle cash

B   As a security measure to check the work of cashiers

C   To assess the sales performance of the organisation

D   As a way of ensuring documentation is being dealt with correctly

148 **What is the double entry to record the reimbursement of the petty cash float?**

A   Debit: petty cash   Credit: cash at bank

B   Debit: expenses   Credit: cash at bank

C   Debit: cash at bank   Credit: petty cash

D   Debit: cash at bank   Credit: expenses

149 DBB Co accounts for petty cash using the imprest system. The following is a summary of DBB Co's petty cash transactions for the week ended 29 August 20X6:

Income	$	Expenditure	$
Opening balance	100	Travelling expenses	54
Sale of stationery	35	Office refreshments	36
Sale of vending machine tokens	20	Cleaning materials	17

What sum should be reclaimed by the accounts assistant at the end of the week?

A $100

B $107

C $48

D $52

150 During the week ended 27 January 20X8, ARK Co acquired significant petty cash receipts when cash takings from office vending machines were emptied. As the petty cash balance is now more than enough to meet normal petty cash requirements, some of the surplus cash will be paid into the bank account.

What is the double entry required to record the payment of petty cash into the bank account?

A Debit: Petty cash   Credit: Bank

B Debit: Expenses   Credit: Bank

C Debit: Bank   Credit: Petty cash

D Debit: Expenses   Credit: Petty cash

PAYROLL

151 For the month of May, the following figures have been extracted from a trader's records with regard to wages.

(i) Employees' social security $678

(ii) Gross basic wages $9,900

(iii) Income tax $2,000

(iv) Employer's social security $925

What will be the total charge for wages and salaries in the final accounts?

A $10,825

B $10,578

C $11,503

D $13,503

152 Qui packs goods on an assembly line. Qui is paid a different amount each week, depending upon the output of assembled goods.

By what method of remuneration is Qui paid?

A   Piecework

B   Commission

C   Hourly paid

D   Salaried

153 Ping and Shan are both paid by piecework. The terms of their employment are:

(i)   Ping is paid $1.15 for each unit produced with a weekly minimum wage of $165.00.

(ii)   Shan is paid $1.10 per unit for each of the first 140 units produced, $1.15 per unit for the next 20 units produced and $1.20 per unit for any additional units.

In a given week Ping produced 135 units and Shan produced 175 units.

What was the gross pay for each employee for the week?

	Ping	Shan
A	$155.25	$195.00
B	$155.25	$210.00
C	$165.00	$195.00
D	$165.00	$210.00

154 **What is the purpose of an income tax code?**

A   To determine the personal allowances available to an employee

B   To determine the amount of employee's social security that must be deducted

C   To determine the amount of employer's social security that must be paid

D   To reflect the tax allowances and reliefs available to an employee

155 Simran and Liu are both hourly paid employees. Their employment conditions are as follows:

(i)   Simran works a basic 40-hour week at an hourly rate of $6.20. Overtime is paid at the rate of time and half for weekdays and double time for weekends.

(ii)   Liu works a basic 35-hour week at an hourly rate of $7.40. Overtime is paid at a rate of time and half for the first 6 hours and double time thereafter.

During a week Simran and Liu both worked for 48 hours, 3 of which were at the weekend.

What is the gross pay for each employee for that week?

	Simran	Liu
A	$331.70	$392.20
B	$331.70	$429.20
C	$381.30	$392.20
D	$381.30	$429.20

156 Aimal and Duha work for an organisation that has a bonus scheme which works as follows:

(i) a bonus of 5% of weekly pay for each employee for any week in which the departmental production is more than 10% above the target production for the week

(ii) a bonus of $1 per employee for every unit of production produced by that employee over 800 per week.

In one week the departmental target was 40,000 units and 45,000 units were produced. Of these Aimal produced 780 and Duha 840. Aimal has a basic weekly wage of $240 and Duha $260.

What is the gross pay for each employee that week?

	Aimal	Duha
A	$252	$313
B	$252	$326
C	$264	$313
D	$264	$326

157 Anish manufactures wooden pallets and employs people on a piece rate scheme of $2.00 per pallet made. If an employee produces more than 200 pallets in a week, any extra pallets made over 200 are paid at a rate of $3.00 per pallet. All employees have a guaranteed minimum weekly wage of $375.

Last week an employee produced 235 pallets.

What was the employee's gross pay for last week?

A $400

B $375

C $505

D $370

158 **How is income tax deducted from employees' salaries accounted for?**

A An asset and a liability

B A liability and an expense

C Income and an asset

D An expense and an asset

159 **How often will a business usually remit income tax to the taxation authority?**

A Weekly

B Monthly

C Quarterly

D Annually

160 What does the labour cost charged in the profit and loss account of a business consist of?

A   Gross pay

B   Gross pay plus employer's state benefit contributions

C   Gross pay less income tax, employee's state benefit contributions and employer's state benefit contributions

D   Gross pay less income tax and employee's state benefit contributions, plus employer's state benefit contributions

161 Rema's annual salary is $15,000. Rema is paid four-weekly and is allowed eight weeks annual leave.

What will be the gross pay on each of Rema's payslips?

A $1,500.00

B $1,363.64

C $1,250.00

D $1,153.85

162 Perani's basic working week is 40 hours, with a basic rate of pay is $7 per hour. Overtime is paid at the rate of time and a half. In a given week, Perani worked 46 hours.

What was Perani's gross pay be for that week?

A $301

B $343

C $385

D $483

163 Dane is a sales representative, selling medical equipment. Dane receives a commission of 2% of all sales plus 0.5% of sales of individual items over $20,000 each, and a further 1% on sales exceeding $70,000 a month.

During July, Dane's sales totalled $90,000, including two large machines with selling prices of $18,000 and $22,000 each.

What commission was paid to Dane for July?

A $4,700

B $4,000

C $2,810

D $2,110

164 Gohar's basic working week is 38 hours, with a basic rate of pay of $7.50 per hour. Overtime hours are paid at 125% of the normal hourly rate.

Last week Gohar worked 44 hours. What was Gohar's gross pay for that week?

A $273.00

B $345.00

C $341.25

D $431.25

165 **Which of the following is NOT a payroll function?**

A   Calculation of gross pay

B   Notification of holiday entitlement

C   Calculation of tax and other deductions

D   Distributing pay slips

166 **By which of the following would it be unlikely to analyse the payroll?**

A   Geographical area

B   Department

C   Home address

D   Factory

167 **Which of the following is NOT used to authorise pay?**

A   Countersigned time sheets

B   Job cards confirmed by managers

C   Self-certified work sheets

D   Weekly time sheets signed by management

168 **An employee believes that an underpayment has been made. How can payroll staff check this?**

A   By asking the taxation authorities

B   By reviewing the payslip provided

C   By asking the employee's manager

D   By looking through the payroll documentation

169 **Which of the following accounts is NOT used in the payroll function?**

A   Bank

B   Drawings

C   Pension payable

D   Wages and salaries expense

SALES AND CREDIT TRANSACTIONS

170 A Co sold goods on credit to the value of $500 (net) to Harper.

In A Co's accounting records, what would be the debit to the receivables' account if sales tax is payable at the rate of 17.5%?

A $412.50

B $500.00

C $587.50

D $606.06

171 A summary of the transactions of Ramsgate, who is registered to account for sales tax at 17.5%, shows the following for the month of August 20X9.

Outputs $60,000 (exclusive of sales tax)

Inputs $40,286 (inclusive of sales tax)

At the beginning of the period Ramsgate owed $3,400 to the taxation authority, and during the period Ramsgate paid $2,600 to the taxation authority.

At the end of the accounting period, what is the amount due to the taxation authority?

A $3,700

B $3,930

C $4,400

D $5,300

172 JKL Co is registered to account for sales tax and issued a sale invoice to a credit customer who is not registered to account for sales tax that had a gross value of $1,200, including sales tax of 20%.

How should JKL Co record this sale?

A   Debit: Receivables $1,200   Credit: Sales $1,000
                                             Sales tax $200

B   Debit: Receivables $1,000   Credit: Sales $1,000

C   Debit: Receivables $1,200   Credit: Sales $960
                                             Sales tax $240

D   Debit: Receivables $1,200   Credit: Sales $1,200

173 IOP Co is not registered to account for sales tax and issued a sale invoice to a credit customer, who is registered to account for sales tax at 20% that had a gross value of $1,800.

How should IOP Co record this sale?

A   Debit: Receivables $1,800   Credit: Sales $1,500
                                                Sales tax $300

B   Debit: Sales $1,800   Credit: Receivables $1,800

C   Debit: Receivables $1,800   Credit: Sales $1,440
                                                Sales tax $360

D   Debit: Receivables $1,800   Credit: Sales $1,800

174 Which of the following statements is true in relation to the sales account?

A   It is credited with the total of sales made, including sales tax

B   It is credited with the total of sales made, excluding sales tax

C   It is debited with the total of sales made, including sales tax

D   It is debited with the total of sales made, excluding sales tax

175 RTY Co is registered to account for sales tax at 10%. RTY Co issued a credit note for $363 to a customer who had returned faulty goods. The customer is not registered to account for sales tax.

How should RTY Co record this transaction?

A   Debit: Returns inwards $330   Credit: Receivables $330

B   Debit: Returns inwards $326.70   Credit: Receivables $363
                Sales tax $36.30

C   Debit: Returns inwards $330   Credit: Receivables $363
                Sales tax $33

D   Debit: Returns inwards $363   Credit: Receivables $363

176 A business sold goods that had a net value of $600 to Lucid plc. The business is registered to account for dales tax at 17.5%.

What entries are required to record this sale?

A   Debit: Receivables $600   Credit: Sales $705
                Sales tax $105

B   Debit: Receivables $705   Credit: Sales tax $105
                                               Sales $600

C   Debit: Receivables $600   Credit: Sales tax $105
                                               Sales $600

D   Debit: Sales $600   Credit: Receivables $705
                Sales tax $105

177 A sales tax registered business issued a sales invoice for goods with a list price of $1,325.00 on which a trade discount of 20% was granted. The goods were rated for sales tax at 10%.

What amount of sales tax was charged on the invoice?

A $106.00

B $132.50

C $238.50

D $119.25

178 Sam is preparing an invoice for the sale of a machine. The list price of the machine is $12,000, which is subject to a trade discount of 10%. The sale is subject to sales tax at 15%.

How much sales tax should be included in the invoice?

A $1,530

B $1,620

C $1,080

D $1.020

179 **Which of the following transactions is a credit transaction?**

A   A sale of goods for cash

B   A sale of goods and the immediate receipt of a cheque

C   A sale of goods with payment due in 60 days

D   The receipt of a cheque for goods sold 40 days previously

180 Rohini invoiced a customer for $700 less 5% trade discount, plus sales tax of 20%.

When the customer pays the invoice, how much will Rohini receive?

A $665

B $798

C $805

D $840

181 **A sale was made for $414 including sales tax charged at 15%. What was the accounting entry to the sales account?**

A   Debit $360

B   Credit $360

C   Debit $414

D   Credit $414

182 Cash of $282 was received from a receivable that had purchased goods on credit for $240 plus sales tax at 17.5%.

What accounting entries are required to record this receipt?

A   Debit bank $282   Credit sales $240

                       Credit sales tax $42

B   Debit bank $282   Credit sales $282

C   Debit bank $282   Credit receivables $240

                       Credit sales tax $42

D   Debit bank $282   Credit receivables $282

183 **What does a debit balance on the sales tax account represent?**

A   An amount of sales tax owing to the tax authorities

B   A sales tax expense to be written off in the statement of profit or loss

C   An amount of sales tax due from the tax authorities

D   Sales tax income to be included in the statement of profit or loss

184 At 1 April, Castro had receivables of $4,529. During the month total sales were $16,540 of which 40% were for cash. Cash received from credit customers during April totalled $7,231.

What was the balance on Casto's receivables' general ledger account at 30 April?

A $1,836

B $3,914

C $5,144

D $7,222

185 During a three-month period, a Suarez made sales of $69,200 plus sales tax at 15%. The balance on the receivables' account at the start of the period was $5,329 and at the end of the period was $4,771. No irrecoverable debts were recorded during this period.

How much cash did Suarez receive from credit customers during the period?

A $68,642

B $69,758

C $79,022

D $80,138

186 Avalon gives customers trade discounts from the standard list price and a 5% cash discount for early settlement of invoices within 7 days of issue. A new customer, Nolava negotiates a 25% trade discount. As Nolava is not expected to take advantage of the early settlement discount terms. Avalon's transactions with Nolava's during June were as follows:

June 12   Sold goods with a $5,000 list price

June 15   Novala returned goods with a $1,000 list price as faulty

June 16   Novala paid half of the net balance outstanding

How much does Nolava owe Avalon at the end of June?

A $1,425

B $1,500

C $2,000

D $2,850

187 **If a credit customer takes advantage of early settlement discount terms, when they were NOT originally expected to do so, how would the settlement discount be accounted for?**

A   It will increase expenses

B   It will be a reduction in revenue receivable

C   It will be offset against discount received

D   It will increase cost of sales

188 Vic sells materials to Fran for $240. Fran manufactures goods from these materials and sells them to a customer, Sam, for $360 plus sales tax. Vic and Fran are sales tax registered traders and the goods rate of sales tax is 17.5%.

How much sales tax is paid to the taxation authorities by each party to the transactions?

A	Vic pays	$42 and Fran pays	$63
B	Fran pays	$42 and Sam pays	$63
C	Vic pays	$42 and Fran pays	$21
D	Fran pays	$42 and Vic pays	$21

189 A business has an opening balance on the sales tax account showing an amount owing to the taxation authorities of $3,210. During the period there were sales of $21,700, excluding sales tax, and purchases of $18,480, including sales tax. During the period $2,890 was paid to the taxation authorities. The standard rate of sales tax is 10%.

What is the balance carried forward on the sales tax account at the end of the period?

A $642 credit

B $810 credit

C $1,042 credit

D $196 credit

190 **Which of the following procedures should help to reduce overdue receivables' balances?**

A   Improved debt collection methods

B   An increase in the bank overdraft facility

C   Credit customers paying invoices more slowly

D   An increase in credit facilities to customers

191 Chay sold goods for $1,200 and bought goods for $810. Both transactions included sales tax at 20% in the prices given.

How much will Chay pay to the tax authorities in respect of these two transactions?

A $38.00

B $65.00

C $78.00

D $390.00

192 **Which one of the following statements best explains what output tax is?**

A   It is a tax on purchases

B   It is a tax on sales

C   It is a payment to the tax authorities

D   It is a repayment from the tax authorities

193 On 1 February the credit balance on Jo's Sales tax account was $2,400. During the month, sales tax on sales was $1,050, sales tax on purchases and other expenses was $900 and a repayment of sales tax was received of $200.

What was the credit balance on Jo's sales tax account at 28 February?

A $2,050

B $2,350

C $2,450

D $2,750

194 **Who normally suffers the burden of sales tax?**

A   The first supplier in the chain of supply

B   The manufacturer

C   The retailer

D   The final consumer

195 During March 20X6 a business made sales of $24,600 and purchases of $15,200 exclusive of sales tax. The business is registered to account for sales tax and both sales and purchases are subject to sales tax at 17.5%.

What is the balance on the sales tax account at 31 March 20X6 if the opening balance was zero?

A   A debit balance of $1,645

B   A credit balance of $1,645

C   A debit balance of $11,045

D   A credit balance of $11,045

196 During a three-month period a business made the following sales and purchases:

Sales $34,800 (exclusive of sales tax at 17.5%)

Purchases $30,785 (inclusive of sales tax at 17.5%)

What is the balance on the sales tax account at the end of the three-month period if the opening balance was zero?

A $598

B $703

C $1,505

D $8,600

197 During a three-month period a business made sales of $72,145, including sales tax at 17.5%, and purchases of $54,200, excluding sales tax at 17.5%. There was an amount due to the taxation authorities at 17.5% at the start of the three-month period totalling $1,354.

What was the balance on the sales tax account at the end of the three-month period?

A $94

B $1,260

C $2,614

D $4,669

198 **At what point should sales tax on a credit sale be recorded?**

A   By the seller when the invoice is issued and by the customer when the invoice is received

B   By the seller when the invoice is issued and by the customer when the payment is made to the supplier

C   By the seller when the cash payment is received and by the customer when the invoice is received

D   By the seller when the cash payment is received and by the customer when the cash payment is made

199   **When must a business charge sales tax on its sales?**

A   If it is a limited liability entity

B   If it sells goods and services

C   If it is registered to account for sales tax

D   If it has been trading for more than one year

200   **Which of the following would be appropriate to write off as an irrecoverable debt?**

A   A cash sale

B   A credit sale made within the last month

C   A credit sale over the organisation's credit limit made in the last week

D   A credit sale within the organisation's credit limit and outstanding for a year

201   **What is the purpose of an aged receivables' analysis?**

A   To monitor the time receivables are outstanding

B   To list irrecoverable debts

C   To hold receivables temporarily

D   To calculate credit limits

202   **Which of the following entries is used to record an irrecoverable debt?**

A   Dr Receivables   Cr Irrecoverable debts

B   Dr Irrecoverable debts   Cr Receivables

C   Dr Profit and loss account   Cr Irrecoverable debts

D   Dr Irrecoverable debts   Cr Profit and loss account

203   **Why would you NOT send a statement to an account written off as an irrecoverable debt?**

A   Doing so would advise the customer there is no need to pay

B   Doing so would encourage the customer to pay

C   It is against the law of contract to do so

D   It is against data protection legislation to do so

204   Ark Co has a debt due from a credit customer of $800. The customer is experiencing severe difficulties and has agreed to return goods that were purchased for $600. Ark Co decided to write off the remaining balance.

What is the double entry required by Ark Co to record this?

A   Dr Account receivable $800; Cr Sales returns $600; Cr Irrecoverable debts $200

B   Dr Irrecoverable debts $200; Dr Bank $600; Cr Sales returns $800

C   Dr Irrecoverable debts $200; Dr Sales returns $600; Cr Account receivable $800

D   Dr Sales returns $800; Cr Irrecoverable debt $200; Cr Bank $600

205 A business sold goods to the value of $500 (net) to Smart.

What would be the debit to receivables if sales tax is payable at a rate of 20%?

A $416.67

B $500.00

C $583.33

D $600.00

206 A summary of the transactions of Sandstone, who is registered for sales tax at 20%, showed the following for the month of May 20X5.

Outputs $80,000 (exclusive of sales tax)

Inputs $64,200 (inclusive of sales tax)

At the beginning of the period Sandstone owed $4.500 to the taxation authorities, and during the period Sandstone paid $3,600 to the taxation authority.

At the end of the period, how much is owing to the taxation authority?

A $2,800

B $4,400

C $6,200

D $13,400

207 A sales tax registered business issued a sales invoice for goods with a list price of $1,480.00. A trade discount of 5% was given. The goods were rated for sales tax at 20%.

What was the gross value of the invoice?

A $1,420.80

B $1,687.20

C $1,776.00

D $1,476.30

208 Farmer is preparing an invoice for the sale of a machine. The list price of the machine is $10,500, on which a trade discount of 8% will be applied. The sale is subject to sales tax at 20%.

What will be the gross value of the invoice?

A $9,072.00

B $10,080.00

C $10,432.80

D $11,592.00

209 Cal makes a sale on credit for $423 excluding sales tax at 20%.

What is the entry to the trade receivables general ledger account?

A   Debit $423.00

B   Credit $507.60

C   Debit $507.60

D   Credit $423.00

210 MAR Co is preparing an invoice for the sale of one of its products. The list price of the product is $14,500, on which a trade discount of 4% was granted. MAR Co has also offered the customer early settlement discount of 5% if payment is made within 14 days. The customer is expected to take up the offer of early settlement discount and pay within 14 days. The sales invoice was prepared on that basis.

What was the gross value of the invoice?

A $13,920.00

B $13,775.00

C $14,500.00

D $13,224.00

211 MAR Co is preparing an invoice for the sale of one of its products. The list price of the product is $2,800, on which a trade discount of 5% was granted. MAR Co has also offered the customer early settlement discount of 10% if payment is made within 7 days. The customer is not expected to take up the offer of early settlement discount.

What was the gross value of the invoice?

A $2,394

B $2,380

C $2,660

D $2,520

212 At 1 July 20X5, Yanlin's allowance for receivables was $48,000. At 30 June 20X6, trade receivables amounted to $838,000. It was decided to write off $72,000 of these debts and adjust the allowance for receivables to $60,000.

What are the final amounts for inclusion in Yanlin's statement of financial position at 30 June 20X6?

	Trade receivables	Allowance for receivables	Net balance
	$	$	$
A	838,000	60,000	778,000
B	766,000	60,000	706,000
C	766,000	108,000	658,000
D	838,000	108,000	730,000

213 On 1 January 20X3 Tipton Co's trade receivables were $10,000. The following information relates to the year ended 31 December 20X3:

	$
Credit sales	100,000
Banked receipts	90,000
Irrecoverable debts written off in year	800
Discounts received	700

Cash receipts include $1,000 in respect of a receivable previously written off.

What was the carrying amount of receivables at 31 December 20X3?

A $21,000

B $21,200

C $19,200

D $20,200

214 A business has been notified that a customer who owed $500 has been declared insolvent. The business had previously made an allowance against this receivable.

What accounting entries are required to account for the amount due from the insolvent customer?

	Debit	**Credit**
A	Irrecoverable debts	Receivables
B	Receivables	Irrecoverable debts
C	Allowance for receivables	Receivables
D	Receivables	Allowance for receivables

215 Headington was owed $37,500 by its customers at 1 January 20X8 and $49,000 at 31 December 20X8.

During 20X8, cash sales of $263,500 and credit sales of $357,500 were made, contras with payables amounted to $1,750 and discounts received totalled $21,400. Irrecoverable debts of $3,500 were written off and Headington wishes to increase its allowance for receivables from $7,500 to $10,000.

What was the cash received from receivables during the year ended 31 December 20X8?

A $339,000

B $342,500

C $340,750

D $344,250

216 Alex had total receivables of $87,000 and an allowance for receivables of $2,500 at the start of the accounting year.

During the year, two specific debts were written off, one for $800 and the other for $550. A debt of $350 that was written off as irrecoverable in the previous year was paid during the year. At the year-end, total receivables were $90,000 and the allowance for receivables was $2,300.

What was the charge to the statement of profit or loss for the year in relating to irrecoverable debts and the change in the allowance for receivables?

A $250

B $800

C $1,200

D $1,500

217 The receivables' account at 1 May had a balance of $32,750. During May, sales of $125,000 were made on credit. Receipts from receivables amounted to $122,500 and contras with the payables' account of $550 were allowed. Refunds of $1,300 were made to customers.

What is the closing balance at 31 May on the receivables' account?

A $33,400 debit

B $34,500 debit

C $36,000 debit

D $37,100 debit

218 A business had receivables of $8,450 at 1 April of $8,450. During April there were credit sales of $19,600, cheques received from receivables of $22,430, sales returns of $1,000 and a contra with a credit supplier of $540.

What was the balance on the receivables' account at 30 April?

A $4,080

B $4,620

C $6,080

D $12,820

219 Mehtab's receivables, which were $500 on 1 July, increased to $700 at 31 July. During that month Mehtab received had cash sales of $280, issued credit sales invoices of $1,900 and credit notes of $170.

How much cash did Mehtab receive from credit customers during July?

A $1,250

B $1,530

C $1,810

D $1,870

220 The following information is available about a business for the year ended 30 September 20X6:

Receivables at 1 October 20X5	$54,550
Receivables at 30 September 20X6	$52,560
Receipts from all customers in the period	$98,460 (including cash sales of $16,838)

Irrecoverable receivables written off during the period $2,000

What was the value of sales on credit for the year ended 30 September 20X6?

A $85,612

B $79,632

C $96,470

D $81,632

221 A credit customer of Astra Co made a payment to settle an invoice. The goods sold by Astra Co had a list price of $250, on which trade discount of 10% was granted. Astra Co is registered to account for sales tax at the rate of 20%.

What accounting entries are required for Astra Co to record the payment from the customer?

	Debit	Credit
A	Cash at bank $220	Receivables $220
B	Cash at bank $225	Receivables $225
C	Cash at bank $300	Receivables $300
D	Cash at bank $270	Receivables $270

222 Opel Co made a cash sale to a customer. The goods sold by Opel Co had a list price of $500, on which trade discount of 10% was granted. Opel Co is registered to account for sales tax at the rate of 20%.

What accounting entries are required for Opel Co to record the sale to the customer?

	Debit	Credit
A	Cash at bank $540	Sales $450 Sales tax $90
B	Cash at bank $540	Receivables $540
C	Cash at bank $550	Sales $450 Sales tax $100
D	Sales $450 Sales tax $90	Cash at bank $540

223 ABC Co sold goods with a list price of $1,000 to Smith which was subject to trade discount of 5% and early settlement discount of 4% if the invoice was paid within 7 days. The normal credit period available to credit customers is 30 days from invoice date. Based upon past experience, Smith has never taken advantage of early settlement terms and has always paid after 30 days.

If Smith subsequently pays within 7 days and is eligible for the settlement discount, what accounting entries should be made by ABC Co to record settlement of the amount outstanding?

A   Debit Cash $950, Debit Revenue $50 and Credit Trade receivables $1,000

B   Debit Cash $950, Credit Revenue $38 and Credit Trade receivables $912

C   Debit Cash $912, Debit Revenue $38 and Credit Trade receivables $950

D   Debit Cash $912, and Credit Trade receivables $912

224 ABC Co sold goods with a list price of $2,500 to Jones which was subject to trade discount of 5% and early settlement discount of 4% if the invoice was paid within 7 days. The normal credit period available to credit customers is 30 days from invoice date. Based upon past experience, Jones always takes advantage of early settlement terms.

If Jones subsequently pays within 7 days and is eligible for the settlement discount, what accounting entries should be made by ABC Co to record settlement of the amount outstanding?

A   Debit Cash $2,280, Debit Revenue $95 and Credit Trade receivables $2,375

B   Debit Cash $2,280 and Credit Trade receivables $2,280

C   Debit Cash $2,375, Debit Revenue $125 and Credit Trade receivables $2,500

D   Debit Cash $2,500, and Credit Trade receivables $2,500

225 ABC Co sold goods with a list price of $4,500 to Black which was subject to trade discount of 5% and early settlement discount of 4% if the invoice was paid within 7 days. The normal credit period available to credit customers is 30 days from invoice date. Based upon past experience, Black always takes advantage of early settlement terms.

If, on this occasion, Black subsequently pays after 7 days and is not eligible for the settlement discount, what accounting entries should be made by ABC Co to record settlement of the amount outstanding?

A   Debit Cash $4,104, Debit Revenue $396 and Credit Trade receivables $4,500

B   Debit Cash $4,275, Debit Revenue $171 and Credit Trade receivables $4,104

C   Debit Cash $4,275 and Credit Trade receivables $4,275

D   Debit Cash $4,275, Credit Trade receivables $4,104 and Credit Revenue $171

226 ABC Co sold goods with a list price of $3,700 to White which was subject to trade discount of 5% and early settlement discount of 4% if the invoice was paid within 7 days. The normal credit period available to credit customers is 30 days from invoice date. Based upon past experience, White does not normally pay early to take advantage of early settlement terms.

If, as expected, White subsequently pays after 30 days, what accounting entries should be made by ABC Co to record settlement of the amount outstanding?

A   Debit Cash $3,515, and Credit Trade receivables $3,515

B   Debit Cash $3,515, Credit Discount received $140.60 and Credit Trade receivables $3,374.40

C   Debit Cash $3,374.40 and Credit Trade receivables $3,374.40

D   Debit Cash $3,515, Debit Revenue $185 and Credit Trade receivables $3,700

227 ABC Co sold goods with a list price of $1,400 to Green which was subject to trade discount of 4% and early settlement discount of 5% if the invoice was paid within 7 days. The normal credit period available to credit customers is 30 days from invoice date. Based upon past experience, Green has always taken advantage of early settlement terms and has always paid within 7 days.

If, on this occasion, Green subsequently pays after 30 days, what accounting entries should be made by ABC Co to record settlement of the amount outstanding?

A   Debit Cash $1,344.00, Credit Trade receivables $1,276.80 and Credit Revenue $67.20

B   Debit Cash $1,400 Credit Trade receivables $1,400

C   Debit Cash $1,344 and Credit Trade receivables $1,344

D   Debit Cash $1,276.80, and Credit Trade receivables $1,276.80

228 Ark Co has a debt due from a credit customer of $784. The customer is experiencing severe difficulties and has now paid $266 in final settlement of the amount due. Ark Co decided to write off the remaining balance.

What is the double entry required by Ark Co to record the cash receipt and irrecoverable debt write-off?

A   Dr Cash at bank $266; Dr Irrecoverable debt $518, Cr Receivables $784

B   Dr Cash at bank $266; Dr Receivables $518; Cr Irrecoverable debts $784

C   Dr Receivables $784; Cr Cash $266; Cr Irrecoverable debts $518

D   Dr Irrecoverable debts $266, Dr Cash at bank $518; Cr Receivables $784

229 Jazz Co has receivables of $43,821 and, within this amount, there are irrecoverable debts of $248 which should be written off. Jazz Co also wishes to increase the allowance for receivable by $500.

What are the accounting entries required to record this?

A   Dr Irrecoverable debts $748; Cr Receivables $500, Cr Allowance for receivables $248

B   Dr Irrecoverable debts $748; Cr Receivables $248; Cr Allowance for receivables $500

C   Dr Irrecoverable debts $518; Dr Allowance for receivables $248; Cr Receivables $784

D   Dr Receivables $248; Dr Allowance for receivables $500; Cr Irrecoverable debts $784

230 Salsa Co has receivables of $27,431 and, within this amount, there are irrecoverable debts of $2,160 which should be written off. Salsa Co also wishes to reduce the allowance for receivables by $350.

What are the accounting entries required to record this?

A Dr Receivables $2,160; Cr Irrecoverable debts $2,160

B Dr Irrecoverable debts $2,160; Cr Receivables $2,160

C Dr Irrecoverable debts $1,810; Dr Allowance for receivables $350; Cr Receivables $2,160

D Dr Receivables $2,160; Cr Allowance for receivables $350; Cr Irrecoverable debts $1,810

231 Samba Co has receivables of $56,134 and, within this amount, there are irrecoverable debts of $1,888 which should be written off. Salsa Co also wishes to increase the allowance for receivables by $175.

What are the accounting entries required to record this?

A Dr Allowance for receivables $2,963; Dr Irrecoverable debts $175; Cr Receivables $2,788

B Dr Receivables $2,063; Cr Irrecoverable debts $2,063

C Dr Irrecoverable debts $2.063; Cr Receivables $2,063

D Dr Irrecoverable debts $2,063; Cr Allowance for receivables $175; Cr Receivables $1,888

PURCHASES AND CREDIT TRANSACTIONS

232 Jai purchased several items of clothing, costing $120, $60 and $190 respectively. These are all gross figures, inclusive of sales tax at 17.5%.

How much sales tax in total did Jai pay?

A $55.11

B $64.75

C $74.48

D $68.51

233 **What accounting entries are required to record a purchase made on credit which cost $350 plus sales tax at 12% by a business registered to account for sales tax?**

A Debit Purchases $350   Credit Payables $392
        Sales tax $42

B Debit Payables $392   Credit Purchases $350
                                      Sales tax $42

C Debit Purchases $392   Credit Payables $392

D Debit Purchases $350   Credit Bank $392
        Sales tax $42

234 WHE returned goods that had a net value of $800 to Rawlins Co. In WHE's accounting records, what would be the value of the debit made in Rawlins Ltd's payables ledger account if sales tax is applicable at the rate of 17.5%?

A $660.00

B $800.00

C $940.00

D $969.70

235 WRE is registered for sales tax and purchased goods that with a net value of $700 plus sales tax at 17.5% on credit from Roper.

What would be the value of the debit to WRE's purchases account?

A $577.50

B $700.00

C $822.50

D $848.48

236 Rivano has a balance of $350,000 on its payables account in the general ledger at 31 May 20X4.

What does this balance indicate?

A   It purchased goods which cost $350,000 in May

B   It is owed $350,000 by its customers at 31 May

C   It owes $350,000 to its suppliers at 31 May

D   It paid $350,000 to its suppliers in May

237 A trader who is not registered for sales tax purposes purchased goods on credit. These goods have a list price of $2,000 and the trader is granted a trade discount of 20%. The goods are subject to sales tax at 17.5%.

What monetary value should be used to record this purchase?

A $1,600

B $1,880

C $2,000

D $2,350

238 A business had sales (including sales tax) of $45,237.50, and purchases (excluding sales tax) of $31,500.00. There was a nil balance on the sales tax account at start of the accounting period.

What was the closing balance on the sales tax account, assuming all items are subject to sales tax at 10%?

A $962.50 credit

B $1,058.75 credit

C $1,248.86 credit

D $1,373.75 credit

239 Goods were returned by Manvi to a supplier that had a net value of $200, on which sales tax of 15% was applicable.

What accounting entries should Manvi make to record this transaction?

A   Debit Payables $230   Credit Sales tax $30
                                                 Returns outwards $200

B   Debit Returns outwards $200   Credit Payables $230
             Sales tax $30

C   Debit Purchases $200   Credit Payables $230
             Sales tax $30,

D   Debit Payables $230   Credit Sales tax $200
                                                 Returns outwards $30

240 **What is the effect of payment of cash to an account payable?**

A   It will increase accounts receivable and reduce cash balance

B   It will reduce cash balance and reduce current liabilities

C   It will reduce accounts payable and increase purchases

D   It will increase accounts payable and reduce cash balance

241 **What the accounting entries are required to record goods returned outwards which had cost $300?**

A   Debit payables $300   Credit returns outwards $300

B   Debit payables $300   Credit returns inwards $300

C   Debit Returns outwards $300   Credit payables $300

D   Debit returns inwards $300   Credit payables $300

242 Nehal received goods from Bren on credit terms and Nehal subsequently paid the amount due by cheque. Nehal then discovered that the goods are faulty and cancelled the cheque before it was cashed by Bren.

How should Nehal record the cancellation of the cheque in the accounting records?

A	Debit payables	Credit returns outwards
B	Credit bank	Debit payables
C	Debit bank	Credit returns outwards
D	Credit payables	Debit returns outwards

243 **Which is of the following is the logical order in which the given documents would appear in a business system?**

A   Purchase requisition, delivery note, purchase order, goods received note

B   Purchase order, delivery note, purchase requisition, goods received note

C   Purchase requisition, purchase order, delivery note, goods received note

D   Purchase requisition, purchase order, goods received note, delivery note

244 **Which of the following is NOT a feature or purpose of a purchase invoice?**

A   To record the amount of the sales tax on the purchase

B   To post the sales tax to the purchases returns ledger account

C   To state the date that payment is due

D   To record the amount and type of goods purchased

245 **Which of the following details would be inappropriate on a purchase order issued by one business to another, both of which are registered to account for sales tax?**

A   Registered office and company registration number

B   Sales tax registration number

C   Quantity and price of goods ordered

D   Sales tax on goods ordered

246 **What is the double entry required to record a purchase on credit?**

A	Debit purchases	Credit receivables
B	Debit inventory	Credit payables
C	Debit payables	Credit purchases
D	Debit purchases	Credit payables

247 If an invoice states that the settlement terms are 'net 30 days', what does it indicate?

A That the invoice amount, net of sales tax, is payable 30 days from receipt of the goods

B That the invoice amount, net of sales tax, is payable 30 days from the invoice date

C That the invoice amount, gross of sales tax, is payable 30 days from receipt of the goods

D That the invoice amount, gross of sales tax, is payable 30 days from the invoice date

248 The closing balance on the trade payables account at 31 August was $3,528. During the month payments made to credit suppliers was $11,583. The opening balance on the trade payables account was $2,660.

What were the credit purchases for the period?

A $10,715

B $11,798

C $12,451

D $13,534

249 The following information is available about a business:

Opening payables	$14,550
Closing payables	$12,560
Payments for purchases in the period	$85,460

Of the payments for purchases, $35,640 was for cash purchases.

What was the cost of purchases on credit for the period?

A $47,830

B $48,810

C $49,820

D $83,470

250 A business had payables at the end of its accounting period of $6,538 and had made purchases during the period totalling $85,400 of which 46% were for cash. The balance on the payables account at the start of the period was $6,711.

How much cash was paid to trade payables during the period?

A $39,284

B $39,457

C $45,943

D $46,289

251 A business which is registered for sales tax had a closing balance on its trade payables account of $4,286. During the period under review, purchases on credit of $25,640 excluding sales tax at 17.5% were made and payments to payables totalled $29,660.

What was the balance at the start of the period on the trade payables account?

A $266

B $3,819

C $4,753

D $8,306

252 **Which of the following accounts would NOT appear in the general ledger?**

A   Motor vehicles

B   Motor repairs

C   Settlement discounts received

D   Trade discount received

253 **What are the accounting entries required to record a discount received?**

A   Debit: Discounts received   Credit: Receivables

B   Debit: Receivables   Credit: Discounts received

C   Debit: Discounts received   Credit: Payables

D   Debit: Payables   Credit: Discounts received

254 Premier Co sold goods on credit to Carlin Co with the offer of a settlement discount. Carlin Co does not normally take advantage of settlement discount terms. However, on this occasion, Carlin does pay early and is entitled to early settlement discount.

How would the settlement of the sales invoice be recorded in Premier Co's accounting records?

A   Debit Bank   Credit   Payables
     Discount received

B   Debit Bank   Credit   Discount received
                                               Payables

C   Debit Bank   Credit   Payables
     Revenue

D   Debit Bank   Credit   Revenue
                                               Carlin Co

255 Premier Co sold goods on credit to Maycee Co with the offer of a settlement discount. Maycee Co does pay early and is entitled to the settlement discount.

How would the settlement of this invoice be recorded in Maycee Co's accounting records?

A	Debit	Payables	Credit	Bank
		Discount received		

B	Debit	Payables	Credit	Discount received
				Bank

C	Debit	Payables	Credit	Bank
		Revenue		

D	Debit	Payables	Credit	Revenue
				Bank

256 Which of the following statements is a good reason to maintain an aged payables analysis?

A To detect potential irrecoverable debts

B To prevent the business missing opportunities to claim discounts and to act as a prompt when determining which payables need to be settled

C To provide a list of accounts payable outstanding

D To identify orders which have not yet been delivered

257 A business offers internet ordering and payment facilities to its customers. A customer purchased goods for $200 plus sales tax at 17.5% and paid by credit card.

How would this transaction be posted to the accounts of the purchaser?

A Dr Bank $200; Dr Sales tax $35; Cr Purchases $235

B Dr Purchases $200; Dr Sales tax $35; Cr: Account payable

C Dr Purchases $200; Dr Sales tax $35; Cr Credit card account $235

D Dr Account payable $235; Cr Credit card account $235

258 What will be the effect on a business if a number of transactions are coded incorrectly and posted within the computerised accounting system?

A The accounts will not be representative of the assets, liabilities, income and expenses of the business

B The accounts will not balance

C The sales and purchases will be mixed up and suppliers' and customers' accounts will be misleading

D The business would be acting illegally

259 For a business registered to account for sales tax, what entries are made in the purchases account?

A   It is credited with the total of purchases made, including sales tax

B   It is credited with the total of purchases made, excluding sales tax

C   It is debited with the total of purchases made, including sales tax

D   It is debited with the total of purchases made, excluding sales tax

260 For a business registered to account for sales tax, what entries are recorded in the sales tax account?

A   It is credited with cash paid to the tax authorities

B   It is debited with sales tax on sales

C   It is debited with sales tax on purchases

D   It is credited with sales tax on purchases

261 Carter purchased goods from Miller that were faulty. What accounting entries are required in Carter's general ledger to account for the return of these goods?

A   Debit: purchase returns   Credit: payables

B   Debit: payables   Credit: purchase returns

C   Debit: sales returns   Credit: payables

D   Debit: payables   Credit: sales returns

262 Roshan purchased goods for $800 less 5% trade discount which were eligible for a settlement discount of 3.5% if paid within ten days. Roshan's supplier is not registered to account for sales tax.

If Roshan pays the invoice to take advantage of the settlement discount, how much will be paid?

A $733.40

B $800.00

C $772.00

D $786.60

263 Who issues a statement of account?

A   A business issues a statement of account to those suppliers it still owes money to, advising them of the amount outstanding

B   A business issues a statement of account to cash customers to advise them how much they have purchased in the previous month

C   A business issues a statement of account to credit customers to advise them how much is the customer owes the business

D   A business issues a statement of account to all credit customers and suppliers to advise them of the amount outstanding or due

264 Which of the following statements relating to a statement of account received by a customer from a supplier is true?

  A   The balance on a statement of account will always agree with the ledger account balance of the credit customer

  B   The balance on a statement of account will never agree with the ledger account balance of the credit customer

  C   The balance on a statement of account will always be higher than the ledger account balance of the customer

  D   The balance on a statement of account can be agreed or reconciled with the ledger account balance of the customer subject to identification of goods in transit, cash in transit, early settlement discount or goods returned

265 The balance on the payables' account was $3,446. It was then discovered that bank payments had been recorded in the general ledger accounts as $14,576 instead of $14,756. A contra with the receivables' account of $392 also needed to be recorded in the general ledger.

What is the amended balance on the payables' account?

  A $2,874

  B $3,234

  C $3,658

  D $4,018

266 The following information is available about a business:

Opening payables	$23,450
Closing payables	$25,600
Payments for purchases in the period	$87,350 (including cash purchases of $17,850)

What is the value of purchases made on credit for the period?

  A $85,200

  B $67,350

  C $89,500

  D $71,650

267 Marty had a trade payables' account balance of $32,750 at 1 May 20X7. During May 20X7, purchases of $125,000 were made on credit, payments made to suppliers amounted to $122,500 and contras with the trade receivables' account amounted to $1,100. During May 20X7, goods which had cost $1,300 were returned to suppliers, for which credit notes were issued.

What was the balance on Marty's trade payables' account at 31 May 20X7?

  A $35,250

  B $35,450

  C $32,850

  D $35,050

268 Ali had a trade payables' account balance at 1 December 20X5 of $52,750. During the year ended 30 November 20X6, Ali made purchases on credit of $325,000, payments made to suppliers amounted to $322,500 and early settlement discounts received totalled $5,250. During the year ended 30 November 20X6, goods returned to suppliers totalled $6,500, for which credit notes were issued.

What was the balance on Ali's trade payables' account at 30 November 20X6?

A $54,000

B $43,500

C $56,500

D $67,000

269 Les had a trade payables' account balance of $34,560 as at 1 July 20X3. During the year ended 30 June 20X4, Les made payments to suppliers of $260,000 and purchases made during the same period amounted to $270,000. During the year ended 30 June 20X4, early settlement discounts received totalled $7,500, and faulty goods returned to suppliers totalled $4,500, for which credit notes were issued.

What was the balance on the trade payables' account at 30 June 20X4?

A $27,560

B $47,560

C $41,560

D $32,560

270 Jools had a trade payables' account balance of $55,555 as at 1 April 20X4. During the year ended 31 March 20X5, Jools made purchases amounting to $395,000. During the year ended 31 March 20X5, early settlement discounts received totalled $6,500, faulty goods returned to suppliers totalled $3,500, for which credit notes were issued. The total on the trade payables' account was $50,555.

What was the total of payments made to suppliers during the year ended 31 March 20X5?

A $390,000

B $397,000

C $403,000

D $410,000

271 A business had a trade payables' account balance of $33,250 as at 1 October 20X2. During the year ended 30 September 20X3, cash paid to settle amounts outstanding for purchases was $335,500. In addition, early settlement discounts received totalled $3,350, faulty goods returned to suppliers totalled $2,500, for which credit notes were issued. At 30 September 20X3, the total on the trade payables' account was $31,750. March 20X5, the total on the trade payables' account was $50,555.

What was the total of purchases made on credit during the year ended 30 September 20X3?

A $339,850

B $333,150

C $334,850

D $328,150

272 Lynx Co purchased goods on credit from a supplier which cost $750, including sales tax at 20%. Lynx Co is not registered to account for sale tax.

How should Lynx Co record this transaction in its general ledger?

	Debit	Credit
A	Purchases $750	Bank $750
B	Purchases $625 Sales tax $125	Payables $750
C	Purchases $625 Sales tax $125	Bank $750
D	Purchases $750	Payables $750

273 Cougar Co purchased goods on credit from a supplier that had a list price of $1,000, before trade discount of 10% was applied. Both the supplier and Cougar Co are registered to account for sales tax at 20%.

How should Cougar Co record this transaction in its general ledger?

	Debit	Credit
A	Payables $1,080	Purchases $900 Sales tax $180
B	Purchases $1,000 Sales tax $180	Discount received $100 Payables $1,080
C	Purchases $900 Sales tax $180	Payables $1,080
D	Purchases $900 Sales tax $180	Bank $1,080

274 Puma Co purchased goods on credit from a supplier that had a list price of $2,400, before trade discount of 5% was applied. Puma Co paid this invoice early to take advantage of the 5% early settlement discount terms offered.

How should Puma Co record the payment in its general ledger?

	Debit	Credit
A	Payables $2,160	Bank $2,160
B	Payables $2,280	Bank $2,166 Discount received $114
C	Payables $2,160	Discount received $240 Payables $1,920
D	Payables $2,400	Discount received $100 Bank $2,300

275 Lion Co purchased goods on credit from a supplier that had a list price of $1,800, before trade discount of 5% was applied. The supplier is registered to account for sales tax at 10%, although Lion Co is not registered.

How should Lion Co record this purchase in its general ledger?

	Debit	Credit
A	Purchases $1,881	Payables $1,881
B	Purchases $1,890	Payables $1,890
C	Purchases $1,710 Sales tax $171	Payables $1,881
D	Purchases $1,800	Payables $1,710 Discount received $90

276 Tiger Co purchased goods on credit from a supplier that had a purchase price of $1,200, after trade discount of 5% had been applied. Both Tiger Co and the supplier are registered to account for sales tax at 10%.

How should Tiger Co record this purchase in its general ledger?

	Debit	Credit
A	Payables $1,320	Purchases $1,200 Sales tax $120
B	Purchases $1,320	Payables $1,320
C	Purchases $1,140 Sales tax $114	Payables $1,254
D	Purchases $1,200 Sales tax $120	Payables $1,320

RECONCILIATIONS

277 After checking the bank ledger account against the bank statement, which of the following items could require an entry in the bank ledger account?

1   Bank charges

2   A cheque from a customer which was dishonoured

3   Cheque not presented

4   Deposits not credited

5   Credit transfer entered in bank statement

6   Standing order entered in bank statement

A   Items 1, 2, 5 and 6 only

B   Items 3 and 4 only

C   Items 1, 3, 4 and 6 only

D   Items 3, 4, 5 and 6 only

278 Which one of the following is NOT a statement which provides an accounting reconciliation or control?

A   Bank reconciliation statement

B   Petty cash imprest system

C   Computerised ledger accounts

D   Trial balance

279 Fatin's bank reconciliation statement shows outstanding lodgements paid in by Fatin of $3,800 and outstanding cheques to suppliers of $3,500. Fatin's bank account in the general ledger shows a debit balance of $25,000.

What balance does Fatin's bank statement show?

A $25,000

B $24,700

C $25,300

D $32,300

280 The balance on the bank ledger account of a business at 30 June was an overdraft of $89.93. At that date there were also unpresented cheques totalling $154.38 and an outstanding deposit of $60.00. It was also discovered that during June the bank had charged the business interest on its overdraft for the previous quarter of $16.45.

What is the correct balance on the bank ledger account at 30 June?

A $73.48 overdrawn

B $106.38 overdrawn

C $167.86 overdrawn

D $200.76 overdrawn

281 The following attempt at a bank reconciliation statement was prepared by Haseen:

Overdraft per bank statement	$38,600
Add: deposits not credited	$41,200
	$79,800
Less: outstanding cheques	$3,300
Overdraft per bank ledger account	$76,500

Assuming the bank statement balance of $38,600 is correct, what was the bank ledger account balance?

A $76,500 overdrawn

B $5,900 overdrawn

C $700 overdrawn

D $5,900 cash at bank

282 Which of the following items would you adjust in the bank general ledger account for when preparing a bank reconciliation statement?

(i) Outstanding deposits

(ii) Unpresented cheques

(iii) Standing order payment omitted

(iv) Bank charges

A (i) and (ii)

B (i) and (iv)

C (i), (ii) and (iv)

D (iii) and (iv)

283 The bank statement shows a balance at the bank of $1,360, whilst the bank ledger account balance on the same date is $1,250.

How could this discrepancy be explained?

A Uncredited lodgement of $110

B Bank charges of $110 not yet recorded in the bank ledger account

C Bank interest received of $55 credited in the bank ledger account

D A dishonoured cheque for $55 which the business did not know about until it was returned, after the date of the bank statement

284 A business has a debit balance on its bank ledger account of $148.00 but the bank statement shows a different balance. The following items were discovered:

(i) the bank statement shows that there were bank charges for the period of $10 which have not been recorded in the bank ledger account

(ii) a standing order payment for $25 has also been mistakenly omitted from the bank ledger account

(iii) cheques totalling $125 had been written and sent to suppliers but had not yet been presented

(iv) a cheque for $85 had been paid into the bank but was still outstanding.

What is the balance on the bank statement?

A $73

B $113

C $153

D $223

285 The bank statement of a business shows an overdraft of $210. Uncredited lodgements are $30 and unpresented cheques are $83. A dishonoured cheque for $28 was included on the bank statement but has not yet been recorded in the bank ledger account.

What is the correct bank ledger account balance?

A $263 overdrawn

B $235 overdrawn

C $157 overdrawn

D $129 overdrawn

286 On 31 December Izaz's bank ledger account shows a balance of $293. The bank statement for 31 December shows a balance of $151.

What could this difference be due to?

A   Uncredited lodgements for which adjustment to the bank ledger account is necessary

B   Uncredited lodgements for which no adjustment to the bank ledger account is necessary

C   Bank interest received as revealed by the bank statement, for which adjustment to the bank ledger account is necessary

D   Bank interest received as revealed by the bank statement, for which no adjustment to the bank ledger account is necessary

287 At 1 March, the bank ledger showed a balance of $850 dr. Transactions during March were:

	$
Cash sales	230
Credit sales	1,950
Cheques written	1,200
Remittance from receivables	1,500

What was the bank ledger balance at 31 March?

A $1,380

B $1,830

C $3,100

D $3,330

288 At 1 April the bank statement showed a balance of $950. Reconciling items in the bank reconciliation statement were unpresented cheques of $100 and a bank error comprising bank charges overcharged to the extent of $20. During April, cheques and deposits appearing on the bank statement were $1,600 and $1,900 respectively. At 30 April, the only reconciling items were unpresented cheques of $210.

What was the bank ledger balance at 30 April?

A $960

B $1,040

C $1,060

D $1,120

289 **Which of the following statements is true in relation to uncredited lodgements?**

A   They constitute an error in the bank ledger account

B   They constitute an error in the bank statement

C   They result from the bank edger being out of date compared with the bank statement

D   They result from the bank statement being out of date compared with the bank ledger

290 **How often should a bank reconciliation statement be prepared for a large retail group?**

A   Annually

B   Monthly

C   Daily

D   Weekly

291 Which of the following items would not affect a bank reconciliation?

A   Dishonoured cheque

B   Discount received

C   Bank interest

D   Lodgements not presented

292 A cheque appears in the bank statement the same day as it appears in the bank ledger. Why would this occur?

A   It has been posted to the payee

B   It has been used to withdraw cash for wages

C   It has passed through the bank clearing system

D   It represents payment to a shopkeeper in a foreign country

293 Which document in a well-run sole trader business should show the same balance as recorded in the business bank ledger?

A   The latest cheque book counterfoil

B   The bank statement

C   The paying in book

D   The petty cash record

294 Which transaction is recorded on the bank statement before the business bank ledger?

A   A cashed cheque

B   Payment of a credit card bill

C   Bank charges

D   A cash sale

295 Which of the following items would not appear in a bank statement?

A   A credit card purchase

B   A debit card purchase

C   A BACS transfer to pay wages

D   An EFTPOS transfer for an internet sale

296 **What is the purpose of producing a bank reconciliation?**

A   To provide assurance that the bank statement contains no errors

B   To provide assurance that the bank ledger account balance is fairly stated and to establish the nature of any timing differences

C   To provide assurance that the bank statement and the bank ledger account is always identical

D   To provide assurance that all transactions entered into by the business are recorded in the general ledger

297 A supplier issued a statement to Pencil Co showing a balance outstanding of $14,350. Pen Co's own records show a balance outstanding of $14,500.

What could be a possible reason for this situation?

A   The supplier sent an invoice for $150 which Pencil Co has not yet received

B   Pencil Co has paid the supplier $150 who has not yet accounted for the cash receipt

C   The supplier has allowed Pencil Co $150 cash discount which is not yet recorded in the general ledger

D   Pencil Co has returned goods worth $150 which the supplier has not yet accounted for

298 XCO Co issued a supplier statement to BVC Co showing a balance outstanding of $14,350. BVC Co's records show a balance outstanding of $14,500.

From BVC Co's perspective, which of the following statements could be a reason that explains this difference?

A   The supplier issued an invoice for $150 which BVC Co has not yet received

B   BVC Co has paid the supplier $150 who has not yet accounted for the cash receipt

C   BVC Co has returned goods worth $150 which the supplier has not yet accounted for

D   The supplier has allowed BVC Co $150 cash discount which has not yet been recorded in the general ledger accounts

299 **Which of the following would be identified by matching a supplier statement against the transactions within the month?**

A   Duplication of invoices

B   Incorrect calculations on invoices

C   Non-delivery of goods charged

D   Incorrect trade discounts

300 A supplier issued a statement of account to Ember Co showing a balance outstanding of $2,850 at 28 February 20X3. Ember Co's payables ledger account for that supplier had a balance of $2,925.

Which of the following reasons could account for this difference?

A   Ember Co has paid the supplier $75 which has not yet been received and accounted for by the supplier

B   Ember Co has returned goods of $75 which the supplier has not yet accounted for

C   The supplier has allowed Ember Co settlement discount of $75 which Ember Co has not yet accounted for in its accounting records

D   The supplier issued an invoice for $75 that Ember Co has not yet received

301 Ordan received a statement from one of its suppliers, Alta, showing a balance due of $3,980. The amount due according to the payable ledger account of Ordan was only $230.

Comparison of the statement and the ledger account revealed the following differences:

1   A cheque sent by Ordan for $270 has not been recorded in Alta's statement.

2   Alta has not recorded goods returned by Ordan $180.

3   Ordan made a contra entry, reducing the amount due to Alta by $3,200, for a balance due from Alta in Ordan's receivables ledger. No such entry has been made in Alta's records.

What difference remains between the two entities' accounting records after adjusting for these items?

A $460

B $640

C $6,500

D $100

302 A supplier sent Lee Co a statement showing a balance outstanding of $14,350. Lee Co's records show a balance outstanding of $14,500.

Which of the following reasons could account for this difference?

A   The supplier sent an invoice for $150 which Lee Co has not yet received

B   The supplier has allowed Lee Co $150 settlement discount which Lee Co has not yet accounted for in its accounting records

C   Lee Co has paid the supplier $150 which has not yet been accounted for by the supplier

D   Lee Co has returned goods of $150 which the supplier has not yet accounted for

303 Why does a business perform reconciliations of individual payables' ledger accounts with statements of account issued by suppliers?

A   It is a legal requirement to perform regular reconciliations of individual supplier account balances with statements provided by suppliers

B   It is a necessary part of the accounting procedures for all businesses registered to account for sales tax

C   It provides assurance that the liability outstanding relating to that supplier is fairly stated in the general ledger

D   It confirms that all payments made to the supplier have been received

304 Why is it important for a business to regularly reconcile its records with external documentation?

A   It enables the business to communicate with the external third party and notify them of errors

B   The use of external documents helps to identify any errors or omissions in the accounting records so that they may be investigated and rectified promptly

C   It guarantees that there are no errors or omissions in the accounting records

D   It confirms that any contra entries with the supplier have been correctly accounted for

305 Tarbuck Co received a statement of account from one of its suppliers, showing an outstanding balance due to it of $1,350. On comparison with the payable ledger account, the following was identified:

• The ledger account shows a credit balance of $260.

• The supplier has disallowed a cash discount of $80 due to late payment of an invoice.

• The supplier has not yet allowed for goods returned at the end of the period of $270.

• Cash in transit of $830 has not been received by the supplier.

Following consideration of these items, what was the unreconciled difference between the statement of account from the supplier and Tarbuck Co's payable ledger account?

A $70

B $90

C $430

D $590

306 **Who issues a statement of account and why is it issued?**

    A   A business issues a statement of account to those suppliers it still owes money to, advising them of the amount outstanding

    B   A business issues a statement of account to cash customers to advise them how much they have purchased in the previous month

    C   A business issues a statement of account to credit customers to advise them how much the customer owes the business

    D   A business issues a statement of account to all credit customers and suppliers to advise them of the amount outstanding or due

307 **Which one of the following statements relating to a statement of account issued by a supplier to a customer is true?**

    A   The balance on a statement of account will always agree with the payable ledger account balance of the customer

    B   The balance on a statement of account will never agree with the payable ledger account balance of the customer

    C   The balance on a statement of account will always be higher than the payable ledger account balance of the customer

    D   The balance on a statement of account can be agreed or reconciled with the payable ledger account balance of the customer subject to identification of goods in transit, cash in transit, early settlement discount or goods returned

308 **What is the purpose of performing a reconciliation of a supplier account balance with the statement provided by that supplier?**

    A   It acts a control to identify and resolve any differences between the individual ledger account for that supplier and the statement of account provided by that supplier

    B   It guarantees that here are no errors in the supplier statement

    C   It guarantees that there are no errors in the supplier ledger account

    D   It confirms that all transactions are recorded correctly in the general ledger

309 Hand Co received a statement of account from one of its suppliers, showing an outstanding balance due to it of $1,650. On comparison with the payable ledger account, the following was identified:

- The supplier has disallowed a cash discount of $25 due to late payment of an invoice.

- The supplier has not yet allowed for goods returned at the end of the period of $570.

- Cash in transit of $875 has not been received by the supplier.

When these issues are resolved, the reconciliation will confirm the payable ledger balance of that supplier.

What was the corrected balance on the payable ledger account?

A $180

B $230

C $205

D $1,055

310 Wrist Co had a balance of $450 on the payable ledger account of one of its suppliers. On reviewing the statement issued by the supplier, Wrist Co identified the following:

- Wrist Co had not yet recorded an invoice for $60 issued by the supplier.

- Cash in transit of $253 has not been received and recorded by the supplier.

When these issues are resolved, the reconciliation between the payable ledger account balance and the supplier statement will be complete.

What was the balance on the supplier statement?

A $823

B $643

C $510

D $257

311 Finger Co had a balance of $834 on the payable ledger account of one of its suppliers. On reviewing the statement issued by the supplier, Finger Co identified the following:

- It had not yet recorded a credit note received from the supplier for $72

- Cash in transit of $76 has not been received and recorded by the supplier

When these issues are resolved, the reconciliation between the payable ledger account balance and the supplier statement will be complete.

What was the balance on the supplier statement?

A $838

B $762

C $766

D $834

PREPARING THE TRIAL BALANCE

312 The following are the general ledger account balances of WER at the start of the year:

	$
Sales	628,000
Cost of sales	458,000
General overheads	138,000
Payables	54,000
Receivables	?
Cash on deposit	61,000
Capital	86,000

What is the missing value for receivables?

A $61,000

B $111,000

C $233,000

D $387,000

313 **Which one of the following errors would be identified by extracting a trial balance in a manual accounting system?**

A A transaction was omitted from the ledger accounts

B The accounting entries for some transactions were reversed, with the debit entry recorded as the credit entry, and vice versa

C Different values were recorded for the debit and credit entries for a transaction

D An expense item has been posted to a non-current asset account

314 Ade posted an invoice for equipment repairs of $240 to the building repairs account.

What journal entry and explanation are required to correct this?

A Dr Equipment repairs $240, and Cr Building repairs $240

Being correction of an error of omission – invoice posted to wrong account

B Dr Building repairs $240, and Cr Equipment repairs $240

Being correction of an error of omission – invoice posted to wrong account

C Dr Building repairs $240, and Cr Equipment repairs $240

Being correction of an error of commission – invoice posted to wrong account

D Dr Equipment repairs $240, and Cr Building repairs $240

Being correction of an error of commission – invoice posted to wrong account

315 Sam posted an invoice for $630 to the stationery account. The credit entry was recorded correctly in the general ledger. The invoice was for advertising.

What journal entry and explanation should be made to correct this?

A   Dr   Advertising $630, and   Cr   Stationery $630

Being correction of an error of omission – invoice posted to wrong account

B   Dr   Advertising $630 and   Cr   Stationery $630

Being correction of an error of commission – invoice posted to wrong account

C   Dr   Stationery $630, and   Cr   Advertising $630

Being correction of an error of omission – invoice posted to wrong account

D   Dr   Stationery $630, and   Cr   Advertising $630

Being correction of an error of commission – invoice posted to wrong account

316 **Which of the following will create an imbalance in the trial balance if all account balances are extracted manually from the accounting system?**

A   Drawings included on the credit side of the trial balance

B   Discounts received included on the credit side of the trial balance

C   Purchases included on the credit side of the trial balance

D   Carriage outwards included on the credit side of the trial balance

317 The following are the year-end balances in Sam's general ledger:

	$
Sales	43,000
Purchases	16,000
Equipment	22,000
Overdraft	8,000
Inventory	19,000
Capital	6,000

What is the trial balance total?

A $43,000

B $57,000

C $63,000

D $114,000

318 A trial balance includes a suspense account that contains has one recorded entry of $200. The transaction it relates to is discount received from credit suppliers. The entry in the payables account was correctly recorded, but the office junior was unsure of which ledger account to use to complete the double entry, and posted it to the suspense account.

What is the correcting journal entry?

A   Dr Discounts received $200,   Cr Suspense $200

B   Dr Suspense $200,   Cr Discounts received $200

C   Dr Discounts received $400,   Cr Suspense $400

D   Dr Suspense $400,   Cr Discounts received $400

319 On reviewing a trial balance, it included a suspense account with a balance of $1,500. You discover that the suspense account was opened to record a single unresolved issue, relating to the purchase of an item of equipment. The purchase invoice did not provide sufficient detail to determine the nature of the expenditure and the accounts assistant recorded one part of the transaction in suspense account and correctly recorded the other part of the double-entry in the payables general ledger account.

What correcting journal is required to clear the suspense account?

A   Dr Non-current asset – equip't $3,000   Cr Suspense $3,000

B   Dr Suspense $1,500   Cr Non-current asset – equip't $1,500

C   Dr Non-current asset – equip't $1,500   Cr Suspense $1,500

D   Dr Equipment repairs $1,500   Cr Suspense $1,500

320 When reviewing the computerised general ledger accounts of Marx Co, the finance director noticed that the accounting entries relating to a contra for $1,425 between the receivables and payables accounts had been coded and processed wrongly. The receivables account entry had been coded with the payables ledger code, and the payables account entry had been coded with the receivables ledger code.

What journal entries are required to correct this error?

A   Dr Payables $1,425   Cr Receivables $1,425

B   Dr Payables $2,850   Cr Receivables $2,850

C   Dr Receivables $1,425   Cr Payables $1,425

D   Dr Receivables $2,850   Cr Payables $2,850

321 When reviewing the computerised general ledger accounts of Engels Co, the chief accountant noticed that an accounting entry relating to rental income received of $2,500 had been processed wrongly. The bank receipt had been correctly accounted for, but the other half of the accounting double-entry was recorded as an entry in the suspense account as the accounts assistant was unsure whether this related to rental income or rent expense.

What journal entries are required to clear the suspense account?

A	Dr Rent expense $2,500	Cr Suspense $1,425
B	Dr Rental income $2,500	Cr Suspense $2,500
C	Dr Suspense $5,000	Cr Rental income $5,000
D	Dr Suspense $2,500	Cr Rental income $2,500

322 Punit extracted a trial balance that included ledger account balances for depreciation expense and accumulated depreciation.

How should these ledger account balances be included in the trial balance?

	Depreciation expense	Accumulated depreciation
A	Debit	Debit
B	Credit	Credit
C	Credit	Debit
D	Debit	Credit

323 The trial balance of Crew Co included ledger account balances for the allowance for receivables and irrecoverable debts.

How should these ledger account balances be included in the trial balance?

	Allowance for receivables	Irrecoverable debts
A	Credit	Debit
B	Debit	Debit
C	Debit	Credit
D	Credit	Credit

324 The trial balance of Force Co included ledger account balances for carriage inwards and carriage outwards.

How should these ledger account balances be included in the trial balance?

	Carriage inwards	Carriage outwards
A	Credit	Credit
B	Debit	Debit
C	Debit	Credit
D	Credit	Debit

325   What is the purpose of producing a trial balance?

A   It confirms that there are no errors in the accounting records

B   It is a preliminary step prior to preparing financial statements to ensure that there are no obvious errors or omissions within the general ledger accounts, although they may still contain errors

C   It confirms whether or not the business has made a profit or loss for the year

D   It confirms the proprietor's capital account balance at the end of the year

326   Why is it good accounting practice to close-off ledger accounts and prepare a trial balance before preparing final accounts?

A   It is a legal requirement to do so

B   It is a requirement of the accounting regulation to do so

C   It is the starting point in the process to deal with year-end adjustments and errors, such as the annual depreciation charge, leading to preparation of the financial statements

D   It confirms that, if there are errors in ledger accounts which comprise the trial balance, they are due solely to omitted transactions

327   Which one of the following errors could not occur in a computerised accounting system?

A   Reversal of accounting entries

B   Error of omission

C   Error of principle

D   An arithmetic error on a general ledger account in arriving at the account balance

328   When processing an expense invoice in the accounting system, Maxi correctly recorded the payable liability but debited the motor expenses account, rather than the insurance account.

What type of error is this?

A   Error of commission

B   Error of principle

C   Reversal of entries

D   Compensating error

329 When processing an invoice for the purchase of a new motor, Maxi correctly recorded the payable liability but debited the motor expenses account, rather than the motors non-current asset account.

What type of error is this?

A   Reversal of entries

B   Compensating error

C   Error of principle

D   Error of commission

330 In which columns in the trial balance should the following general ledger accounts be included?

	Sales returns	Purchases returns
A	Debit	Debit
B	Debit	Credit
C	Credit	Debit
D	Credit	Credit

331 Kim's bookkeeper has posted an invoice for motor repairs to the motor vehicles at cost account.

What term is used to describe this type of error?

A   Error of omission

B   Error of commission

C   Error of principle

D   Error of transposition

332 Andi paid for, and correctly accounted for, van repairs following a road traffic accident. Andi subsequently made an insurance claim and received a direct payment of $450 from the insurance company in settlement of that claim. Andi's bookkeeper recorded the direct payment correctly in the bank ledger account, but recorded the other part of the transaction in the suspense account, pending receipt of further information.

What journal entry is required to eliminate the balance on the suspense account?

A	Dr	Suspense	$450, and	Cr	Insurance	$450
B	Dr	Insurance	$450, and	Cr	Suspense	$450
C	Dr	Suspense	$450, and	Cr	Van repairs	$450
D	Dr	Van Repairs	$450, and	Cr	Suspense	$450

333 Which of the following items would normally be a credit balance in the trial balance?

(i)   Bank loan

(ii)   Owner's capital

(iii)   Drawings

(iv)   Purchases

A   (i) and (ii)

B   (i) and (iii)

C   (ii) and (iii)

D   (ii) and (iv)

334 Which of the following balances would appear on the same side in the trial balance?

A   Drawings and trade payables

B   Drawings and purchases

C   Owner's capital and purchases

D   Owner's capital and rent

335 Which of the following pairs of balances would appear on the same side of a trial balance?

(i)   bank loan and cash in hand

(ii)   Trade receivables and purchases

(iii)   Trade payables and purchases

(iv)   Bank loan and trade payables

A   (i) and (ii)

B   (ii) and (iii)

C   (ii) and (iv)

D   (iii) and (iv)

336 Which of the following statements describes a compensating error?

A   They are not revealed by the preparation of a trial balance and do not require adjustment

B   They are not revealed by the preparation of a trial balance and do require adjustment

C   They are revealed by the preparation of a trial balance and do not require adjustment

D   They are revealed by the preparation of a trial balance and do require adjustment

337 When recording the purchase of goods from a credit supplier, Lime Co posted the gross cost of $1,500 to the purchases and payables general ledger accounts. Both the supplier and Lime Co are registered to account for sales tax at the rate of 20%.

What journal adjustment should Lime Co make to correct this error?

A	Dr	Purchases	$300, and	Cr	Sales tax	$300
B	Dr	Sales tax	$250, and	Cr	Purchases	$250
C	Dr	Sales tax	$300, and	Cr	Purchases	$300
D	Dr	Purchases	$250, and	Cr	Sales tax	$250

338 Peach Co returned faulty goods to a supplier and received a credit note from the supplier. When recording the credit note in the accounting system, Lime Co omitted to account for sales tax and, instead posted the gross amount of $1,296 to the returns outwards account. Both Peach Co and the supplier are registered to account for sales tax at the rate of 8%.

What journal adjustment should Peach Co make to correct this error?

A	Dr	Sales tax	$96, and	Cr	Cash at bank	$300
B	Dr	Sales tax	$96, and	Cr	Payables	$250
C	Dr	Sales tax	$96, and	Cr	Returns outwards	$96
D	Dr	Sales tax	$96, and	Cr	Purchases	$250

339 When recording a contra entry for $2,000 in the general ledger, Lemon Co correctly recorded the entry in the payables account, and recorded the other entry in the allowance for receivables account. Both Lemon and Co and the other party are registered to account for sales tax at the rate of 20%.

What journal adjustment should Lemon Co make to correct this error?

A	Dr	Receivables	$2,000, and Cr Allowance for receivables $2,000
B	Dr	Receivables	$2,400, and Cr Receivables $2,400
C	Dr	Allowance for receivables $2,400, and Cr Receivables $2,400
D	Dr	Allowance for receivables $2,000, and Cr Receivables $2,000

340 When recording a sales invoice for a credit customer, Date Co recorded the net amount as $1,000 instead of $100. Date Co is registered to account for sales tax at 10%.

What journal adjustment should Date Co make to correct this error?

A	Dr	Repairs	$500, and	Cr	Non-current assets	$500
B	Dr	Repairs	$575, and	Cr	Non-current assets	$575
C	Dr	Non-current assets $500, and Cr Repairs				$500
D	Dr	Sales	$900, and	Cr	Receivables	$990
	Dr	Sales tax	$90			

Section 3

ANSWERS TO STUDY SUPPORT QUESTIONS

BUSINESS TRANSACTIONS AND DOCUMENTATION

1 CASH OR CREDIT

TRANSACTION		CASH	CREDIT
(a)	Receipt of goods costing $140.59 from a supplier together with an invoice for that amount.		✓
(b)	Payment of $278.50 by cheque for a purchase at the till.	✓	
(c)	Receipt of a deposit of $15.00 for goods.	✓	
(d)	Sending of an invoice for $135.00 to the payer of the deposit for the remaining value of the goods.		✓
(e)	Sale of goods for $14.83, payment received by credit card.	✓	

2 DOCUMENTS

(a) Order

(b) Purchase invoice

(c) Remittance advice

(d) Credit note

(e) Cash receipt

3 DEBIT/CREDIT NOTES

A credit note is a document produced by the **supplier** and sent to the **customer** which cancels all or part of **an invoice**.

A debit note, on the other hand, is raised by the **customer** and sent to the **supplier** requesting a **credit note**. Not all businesses employ a formal debit note for this purpose; many rely on a letter or telephone call only.

DOUBLE ENTRY BOOKKEEPING

4   TERMINOLOGY

(a)   An **asset** is a present resource controlled by the **entity** as a result of a past **event**.

(b)   A **liability** is an amount owed by the business to another business or individual.

Examples include a **loan from a bank** and amounts owed to the suppliers of goods or services which have yet to be paid for – payables.

(c)   **Inventory** is an asset comprising goods purchased for resale, components for inclusion in manufactured products, and the finished products which have been manufactured which have not yet been sold.

(d)   **Capital** is the liability of the business to the owner of the business.

(e)   **Drawings** is the term which refers to amounts taken out of the business by the owner.

5   CLASSIFYING TRANSACTIONS AND BALANCES

(a)   Asset – inventory

(b)   Expense

(c)   Income

(d)   Asset – trade receivables

(e)   Expense

(f)   Liability (this is a special liability known as capital)

(g)   Liability – payables

(h)   Asset

(i)   Asset

(j)   Income

(k)   Asset

6   BAO SMITH – ACCOUNTING EQUATION

(a)   Bao Smith starts a new business by depositing $10,000 into a business bank account.

Assets =	Capital	+ Profit	– Drawings	+ Liabilities
10,000	10,000			

(b)   A bank lends the business a further $5,000.

Assets =	Capital	+ Profit	– Drawings	+ Liabilities
15,000	10,000			5,000

(c)   Bao buys a delivery van for $6,000.

Assets =	Capital	+ Profit	– Drawings	+ Liabilities
15,000	10,000			5,000

Although the accounting equation looks the same as in (b) above, the assets now consist of cash at bank ($9,000) and van ($6,000).

(d)   Bao buys inventory for $2,500 by writing out a business cheque.

Assets =	Capital	+ Profit	− Drawings	+ Liabilities
15,000	10,000			5,000

Although the accounting equation looks the same as in (b) above, the assets now consist of cash at bank ($6,500), inventory ($2,500) and van ($6,000).

(e)   All of the inventory is sold for $4,000. The money is paid direct to the business bank account.

Step 1   Work out profit

	$
Sales	4,000
Cost of sales	2,500
	———
Profit	1,500
	———

Step 2   Insert into accounting equation

Assets =	Capital	+ Profit	− Drawings	+ Liabilities
16,500	10,000	1,500		5,000

The assets now consist of cash at bank ($10,500) and van ($6,000).

Conclusion

Remember that all of the $4,000 sales proceeds is paid into the bank account.

(f)   Bao pays a business expense of $400 out of the business bank account.

Step 1   Work out new profit

	$
Sales	4,000
Expenses	
Cost of sales	(2,500)
Sundry expenses	(400)
	———
Profit	1,100
	———

Step 2   Insert into accounting equation

Assets =	Capital	+ Profit	− Drawings	+ Liabilities
16,100	10,000	1,100		5,000

The assets now consist of cash at bank ($10,100) and van ($6,000).

(g)   Finally Bao takes $300 out of the business for personal expenses.

Assets =	Capital	+ Profit	− Drawings	+ Liabilities
15,800	10,000	1,100	(300)	5,000

Cash at bank is now reduced to $9,800. The other remaining asset is the van ($6,000).

7   SAMIN'S BOOKS – LEDGER ACCOUNTS

Transactions	Account to be debited	Account to be credited
(a)	Bank	Capital
(b)	Purchases	Bank
(c)	Bank (or cash)	Sales
(d)	Rent	Bank
(e)	Van	Bank

8   CHRIS FINDLAY – LEDGER ACCOUNTS

Cash at bank account

		$			$
(a)	Capital a/c	1,500	(b)	Rent a/c	230
(e)	Sales a/c	240	(c)	Purchases a/c	420
(g)	Sales a/c	16	(d)	Purchases a/c	180
(j)	Sales a/c	50	(f)	Purchases a/c	10
			(h)	Purchases a/c	80
			(i)	Wages a/c	95
			(k)	Sundry expenses a/c	10
				Balance c/d	781
		─────			─────
		1,806			1,806
		─────			─────
Balance b/d		781			

Capital account

	$			$
		(a)	Cash at bank a/c	1,500

Rent account

		$		$
(b)	Cash at bank a/c	230		

Purchases account

		$		$
(c)	Cash at bank a/c	420		
(d)	Cash at bank a/c	180		
(f)	Cash at bank a/c	10		
(h)	Cash at bank a/c	80	Balance c/d	690
		────		────
		690		690
		────		────
	Balance b/d	690		

Sales account

		$			$
			(e)	Cash at bank a/c	240
			(g)	Cash at bank a/c	16
	Balance c/d	306	(j)	Cash at bank a/c	50
		────			────
		306			306
		────			────
				Balance b/d	306

Wages account

		$		$
(i)	Cash at bank a/c	95		

Sundry expenses account

		$		$
(k)	Cash at bank a/c	10		

Tutorial note

It is not necessary to perform the mechanics of balancing an account which contains only one entry as this entry is the balance.

9 JAY FRY – LEDGER ACCOUNTS AND BALANCING

Cash and bank account

	$		$
Capital	10,000	Van	3,600
Sales	110	Van	1,700
Sales	80	Purchases	400
Sales	170	Freezer	260
Sales	50	Purchases	190
		Wages	40
		Drawings	60
		Bal c/d	**4,160**
	10,410		10,410

Capital account

	$		$
Bal c/d	**10,000**	Cash and bank	10,000
	10,000		10,000

Van account

	$		$
Cash and bank	3,600		
Cash and bank	1,700	**Bal c/d**	**5,300**
	5,300		5,300

Purchases account

	$		$
Cash and bank	400		
Cash and bank	190	**Bal c/d**	**590**
	590		590

Sales account

	$		$
		Cash and bank	110
		Cash and bank	80
		Cash and bank	170
Bal c/d	**410**	Cash and bank	50
	———		———
	410		410
	———		———

Freezer account

	$		$
Cash and bank	260	**Bal c/d**	**260**
	———		———
	260		260
	———		———

Wages

	$		$
Cash and bank	40	**Bal c/d**	**40**
	———		———
	40		40
	———		———

Drawings

	$		$
Cash and bank	60	**Bal c/d**	**60**
	———		———
	60		60
	———		———

10 ASSETS OR LIABILITIES?

(a)   Asset

(b)   Asset

(c)   Liability

(d)   Asset

(e)   Liability

(f)   Asset

(g)   Asset

BANKING AND PETTY CASH

11 PETTY CASH PRACTICE

PETTY CASH ANALYSIS

Date 20X4	Receipts $	Voucher/ reference no.	Details	Total payment $	Sales tax $	Office expenses $	Travel expenses $	Postage $	Stationery $	Sundry $
1 Aug	126.58		Balance b/d							
1 Aug	73.42		Cash from bank							
1 Aug		279	Refreshments	11 78		11 78				
1 Aug		280	Taxi	3 90			3 90			
2 Aug		281	Window cleaners	26 00		26 00				
3 Aug		282	Client lunch	27 90	4 16					23 74
3 Aug		283	Stamps	11 00				11 00		
4 Aug		284	Stationery	19 49	2 90				16 59	
4 Aug		285	Rail fare	12 00			12 00			
4 Aug		286	Stamps	2 30				2 30		
				114 37	7 06	37 78	15 90	13 30	16 59	23 74
7 Aug	200		Balance c/d	85 63						
				200 00						
7 Aug	85.63		Balance b/d							
8 Aug	114.37		Cash from bank							

12   IMPREST SYSTEM

Payments out of petty cash will occur when an authorised **petty cash voucher** and supporting **receipts** are produced. Properly evidenced vouchers are **authorised** by senior members of staff.

At the end of the month the petty cash payments will **equal** the vouchers and their supporting documentation, and a cheque will be cashed at the bank for this amount so as to replenish the **imprest**.

The vouchers etc. will be removed and **filed** after having been recorded in the **petty cash summary**. The vouchers, cash and petty cash records are held securely in a box and preferably in a **safe**.

13   BANKING SERVICES

Standing orders and direct debits are both methods of payment whereby the bank is instructed to pay a third party from a bank account. However, the main difference is as follows:

(i)   with a **standing order** it is the payer who instructs their bank to pay a certain amount on a regular basis to the payee

(ii)   with a **direct debit** it is the payee that instructs the bank of the payment and specifies the amount which may alter for each payment.

Credit cards and debit cards are both methods of making payments used by consumers. However the main difference is as follows:

(i)   a **credit card** is a means of purchasing goods without immediate payment. Payment is made on the total balance outstanding on the card sometime after the purchase has been made

(ii)   a **debit card** is a method of making an immediate payment for purchases but without the need to write out a cheque. On payment with a **debit card** the purchaser's bank account is electronically debited immediately with the amount of the purchase.

14   PARTIES TO A CHEQUE

(a)   AM Baker and JS Baker

(b)   National Southern Bank

(c)   L Fuller

15   BANKING MONEY

It is important to keep cash, cheques and vouchers secure. If any are lost or stolen, this may result in financial losses to the organisation. Initially the various items tend to be kept in a **till** and any excess amount should be regularly transferred to a **safe** during the day, keeping actual cash in the **till** to a minimum. Money, vouchers and so on should also be taken to the **bank** regularly to reduce the amount held on premises. This could be daily, every two or three days or other intervals depending on the amount received day to day. The timing of going to the bank should be **irregular** so that there is not a regular pattern of visiting the bank.

Paying in slips are used to include details of cash and cheques and, usually separately, card vouchers. If the business accepts a number of cheques, it is usual to supply a **remittance list** which can be checked against the actual cheques by the bank to avoid or resolve problems.

If the home branch of the business is in another city, the amounts paid into the bank will need to be processed through the **bank clearing system** which may take several days before it reaches the home branch. On receipt, certain items will be 'cleared' such as **cash**. This amount can be used immediately. Cheques paid into the bank are subject to clearance before the amount they represent can be used as cleared funds. This period provides sufficient time for the cheques to be returned if there are any technical problems with the cheque or there are **insufficient funds** in the account.

If the business has a large number of staff, **BACS** should be used to pay wages and salaries into the bank accounts of the staff members. This reduces the amount of cash that needs to be maintained on the premises and avoids the need to write out numerous cheques or credit transfers.

16   MAINSTREAM CO – CHECKING CORRECTNESS OF REMITTANCES

A number of errors have been made on the remittance advice:

(a)   The invoice number **52843** was for **$316.30** rather than the **$361.30** entered onto the remittance advice.

(b)   The revised cheque total should be:

	$
Invoice 52843	316.30
Invoice 53124	227.00
Invoice 53128	450.20

	993.50

17 YANLIN DEMPSTER – BANK LEDGER

(a)

Bank

		$			$
(a)	Capital	10,000	**(d)**	Vans Galore	**2,000**
(e)	Woodside Rugby Club	65	**(d)**	Surgiplast	**150**
			(f)	**Drawings**	130
				Balance c/d	**7,785**
		─────			─────
		10,065			10,065
		─────			─────
	Balance b/d	**7,785**			

(b) The **separate entity** concept is the principle underlying the treatment of the owner's private expenses paid by the business. This concept requires the transactions of a **business** to be recorded separately from those of the **owner** of a business. Consequently, this payment could not be analysed as 'electricity' as it is not the electricity expense of the business. It may be thought of as a withdrawal of cash from the business by the owner.

SALES AND SALES RECORDS

18 SALES TAX

(a)

Sales tax workings	$
Sales	
Net amount	15,790.00
Sales tax $15,790 × 17.5\%$	2,763.25
	─────────
Gross amount	18,553.25
	─────────
Purchases	
Gross amount	12,455.00
Sales tax $12,455 × 17.5/117.5$	1,855.00
	─────────
Net amount	10,600.00
	─────────

Sales account

	$		$
Bal c/d	15,790.00	Receivables (net amount)	15,790.00
	15,790.00		15,790.00

Receivables account

	$		$
		Cash	13,612.00
Sales (gross amount)	18,553.25	Bal c/d	4,941.25
	18,553.25		18,553.25

Purchases account

	$		$
Payables (net amount)	10,600.00	Bal c/d	10,600.00
	10,600.00		10,600.00

Payables account

	$		$
Cash	9,400.00		
Bal c/d	3,055.00	Purchases (gross amt)	12,455.00
	12,455.00		12,455.00

Sales tax account

	$		$
Sales tax on purchases	1,855.00		
Bal c/d	908.25	Sales tax on sales	2,763.25
	2,763.25		2,763.25

(b)   The balance on the sales tax account represents the amount of sales tax that is **owing to** the taxation authorities.

19 VICO LTD – POSTING SALES TRANSACTIONS

General ledger

Sales

	$			$
		30 July	Balance b/d	24,379.20
		3 Aug	Sales listing	986.86

Receivables

		$			$
30 July	Balance b/d	1,683.08	30 July	RCB	1,025.18
3 Aug	Sales listing	1,159.50			

Sales tax

	$			$
		30 July	Balance b/d	352.69
		3 Aug	Sales listing	172.64

Receivables ledger

S Williams & Co				**001**
		$		$
30 July	Balance b/d	38.20		
2 Aug	Sales 5109	69.00		

Montydee					**003**
		$			$
30 July	Balance b/d	73.50	2 Aug	Bank receipt	73.50
1 Aug	Sales 5106	61.48			

Roberts Partners   007

	$		$
30 July Balance b/d	279.30	3 Aug Bank receipt	111.62
2 Aug Sales 5107	153.20		

I Jones   009

	$		$
30 July Balance b/d	137.23	30 July Bank receipt	73.20

Olivia Consultants   015

	$		$
30 July Balance b/d	42.61		
1 Aug Sales 5105	82.47		

A Pargeter   019

	$		$
30 July Balance b/d	198.17	30 July Bank receipt	204.30
2 Aug Sales 5108	221.78		

P Rover   026

	$		$
30 July Balance b/d	296.38		
31 July Sales 5104	142.03		

AM McGee   027

	$		$
30 July Balance b/d	335.28	2 Aug Bank receipt	190.54
Sales 5103	159.30		

P Steven   032

	$		$
30 July Balance b/d	116.78	31 July Bank receipt	116.78

C Brown   035

	$		$
30 July Balance b/d	35.10		
3 Aug Sales 5111	62.70		

Owens Ltd   036

	$		$
30 July Balance b/d	512.74	1 Aug Bank receipt	217.84
3 Aug Sales 5110	159.36		

Cameron Associates   045

	$		$
30 July Balance b/d	335.28	31 July Bank receipt	37.40
Sales 5102	48.18		

20   CREDIT LIMITS

(a)   **Customers exceeding their credit limits**

Name	Account	Credit limit	Current balance
		$	$
P Jones & Co	3419284A	21,000	22,457.75
Smith & Co	7143428B	1,700	1,845.45

(b)   **Customers with credit limits in excess of $20,000**

Name	Account	Credit limit	Current balance
		$	$
ZLT Ltd	1178947A	35,000	17,171.27
P Jones & Co	3419284A	21,000	22,457.75
Cozens & Sons	6143448A	21,000	18,934.21

(c)   Action which can be taken to chase outstanding debts can range from **reminder letters** and **telephone calls** to **legal action** and, eventually, taking a decision to **write the amount off as a bad debt**. Such action must be seriously considered and appropriately authorised by management.

21   LANCING CO – AGED RECEIVABLES ANALYSIS

Aged receivable listing

Customer	< 30 days	< 60 days	< 90 days	> 90 days	Total
	$	$	$	$	$
Vinehall	72.48	–	28.36	53.81	154.65
Cranbrook	227.71	–	128.27	–	355.98
Skinners	–	265.39	103.46	55.35	424.20
Bickley	61.32	39.37	–	–	100.69
	361.51	304.76	260.09	109.16	1,035.52

Tutorial note

Where possible, you should match a payment to an invoice. For example, Cranbrook's payment on 25 February for $117.25 and so clearly relates to the invoice dated 15 February. Where it is not possible to match a payment to an invoice, for example where a receivable has only made a part payment, the payment should be allocated to the earliest outstanding invoice.

PURCHASES AND PURCHASE RECORDS

22   POSTING CREDIT TRANSACTIONS

Transactions	Account to be debited	Account to be credited
(a)	Bank	Capital
(b)	Purchases	Accounts payable
(c)	Purchases	Bank
(d)	Rent	Bank
(e)	Accounts receivable	Sales revenue
(f)	Bank	Sales revenue
(g)	Wages	Bank
(h)	Bank	Loan
(i)	Furniture	Accounts payable
(j)	Bank	Accounts receivable
(k)	Accounts payable	Bank

23 SETTLEMENT DISCOUNTS

Accounts receivable

	$		$
Sales	873	Cash at bank account	873

Sales account

	$		$
		Accounts receivable	873

Accounts payable

	$		$
Cash at bank account	582	Purchases of inventory	600
Discounts received	18		

Discounts received account

	$		$
		Accounts payable	18

Purchases account

	$		$
Accounts payable	600		

Cash at bank account

	$		$
Accounts receivable	873	Accounts payable	582

24 GEER & CO – POSTING PURCHASES TRANSACTIONS

GENERAL LEDGER:

Purchases

		$		$
8 May	Balance b/d	1,652.30		
12 May	Purchases listing	388.00		

Payables

		$				$
			8 May	Balance b/d		912.36
12 May	Bank	477.20	12 May	Purchases listing		455.87

Sales tax

		$				$
12 May	Purchases listing	67.87	8 May	Balance b/d		80.41

PAYABLES LEDGER:

AD Gosling   003

	$			$
		8 May	Balance b/d	21.73
		12 May	Purchases listing 02268	28.70

Rutland Ltd   006

		$			$
12 May	Bank 03365	149.37	8 May	Balance b/d	149.37

Hopkins Ltd   008

		$			$
12 May	Bank 03363	102.64	8 May	Balance b/d	198.37
				Purchases listing G228	128.39

BA Johnson   012

	$			$
		8 May	Balance b/d	–
		9 May	Purchases listing 2294	33.71

PGE Ltd   015

		$			$
12 May	Bank 03366	93.70	8 May	Balance b/d	117.38
			10 May	Purchases listing 29145	105.29

				Flute Brothers		**017**
		$				$
			8 May	Balance b/d		88.29
			9 May	Purchases listing 82456		48.26

				Brass & Co		**021**
		$				$
8 May	Bank 03362	37.90	8 May	Balance b/d		37.90
			10 May	Purchases listing X8/09		51.26

				SC Basson		**023**
		$				$
10 May	Bank 03364	93.59	8 May	Balance b/d		93.59

				Priddle & Sons		**025**
		$				$
			8 May	Balance b/d		–
			12 May	Purchases listing 0135		60.26

25 RETURNING GOODS

Hansa must check that the recollection of memory of the order is correct by referring to the **original order**. This could be a copy of a **written** order, a note of a **telephone** order or an **email** confirmation of an order made over the internet. If Hansa is correct, the supplier should be **contacted** to ensure that the correct goods are delivered and the unwanted items taken back. If there is a delay in delivering the correct goods, Hansa should ask the supplier to provide a **credit note** so that there will not be a charge for the unwanted goods.

PAYROLL

26 PAYROLL KNOWLEDGE

(a)   True.

(b)   False – but only just! Most employees are entitled to a written statement, but in a few cases, e.g. employees working less than one month – this is not necessary. (The legislation may be different in various countries outside the UK.)

(c)   False. Certain responsibilities are implicit, even if they are not stated in the written contract. For example, the duty to exercise reasonable care and skill whilst performing work tasks and responsibilities.

(d)   False, for example: such records must be maintained for at least three years in the UK.

27   GROSS PAY – SALARIED AND PIECEWORK

(a)   Kadal's salary increase occurred two thirds of the way through the month. The gross pay for June is calculated as follows:

	$
$\frac{1}{12} \times \$8,500 \times \frac{2}{3}$	472.22
$\frac{1}{12} \times \$9,000 \times \frac{1}{3}$	250.00
	722.22

(b)   Lahari's production is 630 units. The gross pay is:

$\frac{630}{10} \times \$0.85 =$ **$53.55**

(c)   Lahari's production is 700 units. The gross pay is:

		$
Basic pay	$\frac{700}{10} \times \$0.85$	59.50
Bonus (50 units)	$\frac{50}{10} \times \$1.05$	5.25
		64.75

28   GROSS PAY – OVERTIME

(a)   Paragun's hourly rate of pay is:

$\$14,820 \times \frac{1}{52} \times \frac{1}{37.5}$ = $7.60. The overtime rate is $7.60 × 1.5 = $11.40

	$
The gross pay for the week is:	
Basic pay $14,820 × $\frac{1}{52}$	285.00
Overtime hours (9 – 5) @ $11.40	45.60
Gross pay	330.60

(b)   (i)   Overtime pay = 7 × $5.20 × 1.5 = $54.60

      (ii)   Overtime pay:

	$
4 hours @ ($5.20 × 1.25)	26.00
3 hours @ ($5.20 × 1.5)	23.40
	49.40

      (iii)   Overtime rate   = $10,010 × $\frac{1}{52} \times \frac{1}{35}$ = $5.50

             Overtime pay   =   7 × $5.50 = $38.50

29   PAYSLIP

Your answer may include:

(a)   the employer's name

(b)   the employee's name and tax information

(c)   the date

(d)   the total gross pay for this pay day and to date

(e)   the total tax paid for this pay day and to date

(f)   the net pay.

30   PAYROLL ACCOUNTS

Your answer should mention the cash at bank account. Other general ledger accounts will depend upon the systems used and the legislation in the country in which the payroll is prepared. Typical accounts in your answer might be:

(a)   wages and salaries expense

(b)   wages and salaries liability

(c)   the tax authorities' liability

(d)   pension payable

(e)   various non-statutory deductions.

BANK RECONCILIATIONS AND THE INITIAL TRIAL BALANCE

31   PHILPOTT AND SONS – SELECTING TRANSACTIONS FOR BANK RECONCILIATION

(a)   Adjustment to the **bank ledger** is required: the standing order has been omitted.

(b)   **Reconciling item**: this is an unpresented cheque at 31 October.

(c)   Adjustment to the **bank ledger** required: the customer's bank have not honoured this cheque. Therefore the cheque has been returned to Philpott and Sons' bank who have reduced Philpott and Sons' bank balance accordingly. Philpott and Sons did not know about the cheque at 31 October and so will need to amend its records by making a credit entry in the **bank ledger**. This credit will thus cancel the original debit made on receipt of the cheque.

(d)   **Reconciling item**: this is a bank error; the bank should be contacted immediately to correct this mistake.

(e)   **Reconciling item**: these lodgements were outstanding at 31 October.

32   PREPARING A BANK RECONCILIATION STATEMENT

(a)   **Bank reconciliation statement at 31 May 20X4**

	$
Balance per bank statement	1,434.41
Less: Unpresented cheques	(394.67)
	1,039.74
Add: Outstanding lodgements	936.03
Balance per bank ledger account (working)	1,975.77

Working:

Cash at bank

	$		$
Balance b/d	2,369.37	**Direct debit payment**	**393.60**
		Balance c/d	**1,975.77**
	2,369.37		**2,369.37**
Balance b/d	**1,975.77**		

(b)   The regular preparation of bank reconciliations serves as a **check** on both the organisation's records and those of the bank.

The bank reconciliation may highlight **differences** between the bank statement and the bank ledger account and these can then be **investigated** and the organisation's and bank's records **brought up to date**.

Bank reconciliations also serve as a check on the time taken to bank lodgements and for them to **clear** through the banking system.

Finally cheques that have been drawn but not yet **presented** can also be monitored in this way.

33 HUAN MARSHALL – LEDGER ACCOUNTS AND TRIAL BALANCE

Workings:

Cash and bank account

	$		$
Capital	6,200	Rent	180
Sales	52	Wages	56
Receivables	215	Purchases	66
Loan	1,000	Payables	237
		Drawings	100
		Bal c/d	6,828
	–––––		–––––
	7,467		7,467
	–––––		–––––

Capital account

	$		$
Bal c/d	6,200	Cash and bank	6,200
	–––––		–––––
	6,200		6,200
	–––––		–––––

Sales account

	$		$
		Receivables	441
		Receivables	118
		Cash	52
Bal c/d	708	Receivables	97
	–––––		–––––
	708		708
	–––––		–––––

Receivables account

	$		$
Sales	441	Cash and bank	215
Sales	118		
Sales	97	Bal c/d	441
	–––––		–––––
	656		656
	–––––		–––––

Purchases account

	$		$
Payables	237		
Payables	162		
Cash and bank	66	Bal c/d	465
	–––––		–––––
	465		465
	–––––		–––––

Payables account

	$		$
Cash	237	Purchases	237
Bal c/d	162	Purchases	162
	–––––		–––––
	399		399
	–––––		–––––

Rent account

	$		$
Cash and bank	180	Bal c/d	180
	–––––		–––––
	180		180
	–––––		–––––

Wages account

	$		$
Cash and bank	56	Bal c/d	56
	–––––		–––––
	56		56
	–––––		–––––

Drawings account

	$		$
Cash and bank	100	Bal c/d	100
	–––––		–––––
	100		100
	–––––		–––––

Loan account

	$		$
Bal c/d	1,000	Cash and bank	1,000
	–––––		–––––
	1,000		1,000
	–––––		–––––

Trial balance as at...

	$	$
Cash and bank	6,828	
Capital		6,200
Sales		708
Receivables	441	
Purchases	465	
Payables		162
Rent	180	
Wages	56	
Drawings	100	
Loan		1,000
	8,070	8,070

34 ERROR CORRECTION – JOURNAL

		JOURNAL		
	Date	**Details**	**Dr** $	**Cr** $
(a)	3/3/X5	**Receivables' ledger – P James**	145.79	
		Receivables' ledger – P Jones		145.79
(b)	3/3/X5	Receivables	**282.00**	
		Sales tax		**42.00**
		Sales		**240.00**
(c)	3/3/X5	Sales	**9.00**	
		Receivables		**9.00**
(d)	3/3/X5	G Fletcher – **payables** ledger account	250.00	
		G Fletcher – **receivables** ledger account		250.00
		Payables	250.00	
		Receivables		250.00
(e)	3/3/X5	**Irrecoverable debt expense**	269.47	
		Receivables		269.47

Section 4

ANSWERS TO MULTIPLE-CHOICE QUESTIONS

BUSINESS TRANSACTIONS AND DOCUMENTATION

1 A

Selling provides profit for organisations and credit sales normally occur frequently. Payments to suppliers tend to be carried out once or twice a month. Employees are paid weekly and/or monthly and equipment purchases are infrequent.

2 B

Many business transactions are on credit terms or are settled by cheque. However, some small transactions, such as for local purchases of stationery, are best made by cash. The petty cash system is used in these circumstances.

3 D

A credit note is issued in respect of returned or damaged goods. In these circumstances the amount the customer needs to pay must be reduced. The credit note identifies the amount of the reduction.

4 B

The delivery note is sent with the goods to the customer. It lists the contents of the delivery. The other items are used internally for accounting and other purposes.

5 A

The remittance advice accompanies the cheque to settle an outstanding amount.

6 A

The purchase invoice is received from the supplier and indicates the amount owed for goods or services supplied. It will detail the goods and/or services supplied and contain sales tax details.

7   B

The goods received note is an internal document which contains the details of the delivery note but in a standard form used within the business accepting the goods. The next stage is to be charged for the goods and the amount to be paid is detailed on the invoice. The statement follows the invoices and credit notes for the month. The advice note indicates the goods are coming and arrives before the delivery note.

8   C

Salal is the purchaser who is being advised of the amount that needs to be paid by the invoice from the supplier. When Salal has paid, the supplier will normally send a receipt to acknowledge payment. A credit note would arise if there was a problem with the paper and Salal returned all or part of it. A goods received note is an internal record of goods delivered.

9   D

The petty cash voucher acts as a source document for petty cash transactions. It is signed by the person making the payment or asking for reimbursement and is commonly authorised by an appropriate person in the organisation. Evidence of the expenditure (such as a till receipt, a rail or bus ticket) is often stapled to the voucher. An invoice is used for credit transactions but not petty cash. Money should not be borrowed from petty cash so no IOU should appear in the petty cash records.

10   B

A paying in slip records the amount paid into the bank account and acts as a source document to update the bank general ledger account. Delivery notes and goods received notes details quantities of products and not financial details so are not source documents. A statement is confirmation of transactions and includes details of source documents.

11   D

Once the cheque requisition has been authorised a cheque may be sent. The cheque will be sent with a remittance advice. Debit and credit notes are used to indicate an under or overcast on an invoice, for example.

12   B

The payslip indicates the gross and net pay of an employee as well as detailing any deductions for tax, national insurance and other adjustments to wages and salaries. An advice slip is used to advise a customer that goods/services are due to be delivered. A purchase order may be placed with a supplier to order goods/services, but not with an employee. A quotation is an indication of the cost of a job.

13   C

Invoices tend to generally be headed 'Invoice'. They are a purchase invoice to a customer and sales invoice to the supplier. Credit and debit notes are specific documents used to correct errors, for example. A receipt is given by a supplier to a customer to indicate payment has been made.

14   C

Tax law requires businesses to keep records of purchases, sales, payments to employees, and so on, for a number of years in case there is a need to investigate the affairs of the organisation. Some documents may be kept because a business wishes to build an historic record of its progress but there is no requirement for this to take place. Past performance may or may not help with forecasting, but keeping documents for planning is not a requirement.

15   C

Data protection legislation is designed to protect the individual against information being kept for other than legitimate reasons. Certain information kept about employees for tax purposes, for example, is legitimately kept. Any information recorded about individuals is subject to data protection and other legislation.

16   D

Personal data maintained for domestic purposes is excluded as data protection laws typically apply to businesses. This may include contact details and other personal information relating to friends and family. Personal data of customer and suppliers who are 'natural persons' rather than corporate bodies, is also covered by typical data protection law.

17   C

18   D

19

	True/False
With a cloud accounting system, an accountant or auditor can be granted remote access to data and information they require	True
With a cloud accounting system all employees are granted access to all data and information in the system	False

An accountant or auditor can be granted access to the cloud accounting system to enable them to prepare information and documents, such as sales tax returns or the annual financial statements. Not all employees will have access to all parts of the system. For example, access to payroll data and information is likely to be restricted to staff having responsibility for processing and management of the payroll.

20   B

Coding involves recording an account number for each ledger account. The numbers or codes are then used to post the source documents to the appropriate general ledger accounts.

21   C

Purchases and sales tax are debited and payables account is credited. The use of codes simply replaces ledger account names with numbers.

22 D

Debit Receivables (code 5000) with the gross amount of $528.75. Credit Sales (code 3500) $450.00 and credit sales tax (code 2468) $78.75

23 B

24 D

25 C

26 B

27 D

28 C

29 A

30 D

31 D

32 B

DUALITY OF TRANSACTIONS AND THE DOUBLE-ENTRY SYSTEM

33 B

Taaj introduced $5,000 into the business and as a result cash at bank (an asset) is increased. The cash account has the debit entry (increase in asset). The capital account has the credit entry, since increases in capital are always credited to the capital account.

34 C

As in the previous question, this transaction records an increase in assets (car account) and an increase in capital.

35 C

The $900 is a debit balance because the total value of debit entries ($1,750) exceeds the total value of credits ($850). The balance b/d is therefore a debit balance.

36 C

An increase in capital and an increase in liability both require credit entries in the appropriate accounts. Debits and credits must match each other.

37   D

The accounting equation is Assets = Capital + Liabilities. So, we can have:

Assets ($14,000) = Capital ($10,000) + Liabilities ($4,000)

38   D

Receipts are always debits in the cash a bank account. As a receivable account exists from selling on credit, the receivable is credited to complete the double entry and reduce the amount outstanding from the customer.

39   B

	$
Closing capital	4,500
Opening capital	(10,000)
Decrease in net assets	(5,500)
Drawings: profit taken out	8,000
Capital introduced	(4,000)
Loss for the year	(1,500)

40   C

Debit balances will be assets or expenses. Credit balances will be income or capital.

41   D

The motor van account is used to record this expenditure on assets. The supplier is an account payable to the organisation until the amount outstanding is paid.

42   A

When the cash or bank account is reduced, it is credited in the accounts of the business. Drawings are, therefore, debited.

43   B

The inventory account is updated only at the end of the year when an inventory count and valuation takes place. When inventory is purchases, the cost is debited to the purchases account. When it is sold, the sale is credited to the sales account. Receipts are recorded on the debit side of the cash at bank account.

44   C

Electricity is an expense. Assets and expenses accounts have debit balances. The remainder are examples of income and liabilities which have credit balances.

45   D

Trade payables are short-term liabilities. All liabilities have credit balances. The other items are drawings, an expense and an asset, all of which have debit balances.

46   A

A receipt in cash is a debit to the cash book. When the customer is sold goods on credit, this creates an account receivable balance. So when the receivable pays the amount outstanding, the account receivable account is credited.

47   C

The separate entity principle relates to the business and its owner. Separate entity recognises the difference between them. A and B focus on different aspects of the accounts but are within the business. There is a clear separation between owner of a business and a lender.

48   C

A bank overdraft is a liability as technically it is repayable whenever the bank demands. Accounts receivables and inventories are assets, and drawings represent a withdrawal of capital.

49   A

Petty cash, the salesman's motor car and computer software are all examples of assets. The owner is a liability representing the amount the business owes its owner.

50   D

This is a variation on the conventional accounting equation. Opening capital plus profit less drawings is the closing capital after a period of trading.

51   A

Drawings represent cash and goods withdrawn. Withdrawals by an owner are not classified as an expense, to prevent manipulation of profit by the owner. Inventory represents goods held for resale. A liability is an amount owed by the business.

52   D

The assets of the business are separate from those of the owner.

53   A

A purchase of inventory on credit increases assets and liabilities. There is an equal effect on current assets and current liabilities, so net assets remain the same. Capital is not affected until the inventory is sold for a profit or loss. Then, at that stage, the capital will change.

54   B

Cash, an asset, decreases. Expenses are charged against income, thus reducing profit.

55   B

The general ledger contains the accounts which are not specific personal accounts for credit customers and credit suppliers. Details of non-current assets are maintained in the non-current asset register.

56   D

It is an individual account within the general ledger that contains a record of transactions assigned to a particular item, such as the sales account or the wages expense account.

57   C

The payables' ledger contains the accounts of all credit suppliers. Customer accounts are held in the receivables' ledger. Details of credit limits and personal details may be maintained in the payables' ledger, but it is not a requirement. However, in computerised accounting systems it is customary to record such information when setting up the ledger account for the supplier in the records. Note that the payables' and receivables' ledgers is memorandum only information and they do not form part of the double-entry bookkeeping process.

58   B

Income and capital have credit balances. Expenses and drawings, together with assets, have debit balances.

59   A

Anything which represents the purchase of a non-current asset or which significantly improves a non-current asset is an example of asset expenditure. Day-to-day expenditure, which will be used up within a year, is an expense.

60   C

(i), (ii) and (iv) will all last for a period longer than a year and represent investment by the business in non-current assets and asset expenditure. Repairs simply maintain the computer operating and are an expense.

61   C

(ii), (iii) and (iv) are running expenses needed to operate the business day to day and are expenses. The purchase of a delivery van represents asset expenditure on a non-current asset to be used in the business for more than one year.

62   A

The cost of a non-current asset includes expenses required in its purchase, such as legal costs, installation costs and so on. All of these are asset expenditure. Rent and repairs are expenditure on day-to-day business expenses. Introducing capital is not expenditure.

63 D

The chairs are inventory and will not remain in the business for very long. The delivery van and office building are long lasting and classified as asset expenditure. Tax is an amount owed to a government body and does not represent day-to-day or long-term expenditure for the business itself. It is classed as an appropriation of profit.

64 A

The bank deposit account is an asset. The bank overdraft and lank loan represent examples of liabilities. The capital account represents an amount due by the business to the proprietor, although it is not regarded as a business liability.

65 A

Capital is a liability which the business owes to the owner and is not asset expenditure.

66 B

The account is balanced by introducing a credit transaction (balance c/d) and the double entry is a debit balance b/d. This ensures the balance remains as a debit balance.

67 A

The account is balanced by introducing a debit transaction (balance c/d) and the double entry is a credit balance b/d. This ensures the balance remains as a credit balance.

68 B

Cash is an asset and a bank overdraft is a liability, so the cash balance will be a debit and the bank overdraft a credit.

69 D

Equipment asset at cost

	$		$
Balance b/d	1,000	Bank (disposal/sale)	800
Bank (purchase)	1,000	Balance c/d	1,200
	2,000		2,000
Balance b/d	1,200		

70   C

Machinery asset at cost				
	$			$
Balance b/d	2,000	Bank (disposal/sale)		1,800
Bank (purchase)	2,000	Balance c/d		2,200
	———			———
	4,000			4,000
	———			———
Balance b/d	2,200			

71   B

	$
Opening capital	20,000
Capital introduced	4,000
	———
	24,000
Drawings:	(15,000)
	———
	9,000
Profit for the year (bal fig)	14,000
	———
Closing capital	23,000
	———

72   B

Assets and expenses are debit balances. Income and liabilities are credit balances.

73   B

This double entry correctly records an asset purchased and reduction of the cash account.

74   C

This double entry correctly records an increase in the cash at bank account and an increase in the ownership interest.

75   D

This double entry correctly records a reduction in the liability to the supplier and a reduction in the cash at bank account.

76   C

Drawings and capital introduced represent transactions between the proprietor and the business. Inventory is an asset.

77   D

Computer equipment, petty cash balance and office photocopier are examples of assets. Computer maintenance is an expense.

78   B

The purchase of a car for the business, whether it is new or second-hand, is an example of asset expenditure. Repairs and insurances costs are examples of expenses.

79   C

The purchase of the printer is an example of capital expenditure. All other items are examples of expenses.

80   B

The purchase of a delivery van represents asset expenditure as the van would be expected to be used in the business for a number of years. Painting and decoration of the office is an example of an expense.

81   D

82   A

83   D

Opening capital + profit – drawings = Closing capital. The accounting equation states that proprietor's capital = net assets. Therefore, closing net assets = closing capital.

84   B

85   A

86   C

87   B

The receipt from a credit customer would lead to an increase in cash at bank and a reduction in receivables. The net position is that total assets have not changes. Cash injected into the business would increase assets (cash ant bank) and also the owner's capital account. Settlement of the amount due to the supplier would reduce the cash at bank balance. The purchase of a machine would increase assets.

88   A

89   C

90   A

91   D

92 C

93 B

94 A

95 C

96 B

97 B

98 C

99 D

100

	Selected answer
Statement of financial position	Correct
Bank statement	
Statement of profit or loss	Correct
Supplier statement	

BANK SYSTEM AND TRANSACTIONS

101 C

Using supplier name only may still create inefficiencies when trying to locate individual invoices if the supplier in question is a major supplier of the organisation. Similarly, using purchase invoice date only is likely to be inefficient if there are lots of purchase invoices with the same date. Each supplier will have its own sales invoice sequential order or reference system (i.e. the purchase invoice number from your perspective) – again, not a sensible method of filing and retaining purchase invoices Using both supplier name in alphabetical order and invoice date will be the most effective filing method.

102 A

All of the options stated are disadvantages of not having a document retention policy.

103 B

Many organisations operate a single sequential order filing system for sales invoices. This enables individual sales invoices to be located relatively easily. The other options available lack precision as a system of filing and are therefore relatively inefficient.

104 C

The value of a sale may be recorded on a sales order or a sales invoice. Confirmation that goods have been received will be recorded on a delivery note received from the supplier at the time of delivery. Evidence of payment will be recorded in the cash at bank ledger account and on a remittance advice. A purchase requisition will record the nature and quantity of goods required, and signed by a responsible person to confirm that they are a required for a valid business purpose.

105 D

All four options are advantages of having a document retention policy.

106 B

Cash at bank account

	$		$
Cash sales	900	Balance b/d	500
		Balance c/d	400
	900		900
Balance b/d	400		

107 B

Payment is due in the future so this is a credit transaction and not a cash transaction. The other options are all immediate and involve cash or bank, so are cash transactions.

108 D

A remittance advice provides information of what the payment constitutes e.g. which invoices have been paid. It is not the payment itself.

109 A

The drawer is the person signing the cheque. The drawee is the bank on which the cheque is drawn. The payee is the person to whom the cheque is made out. The payer is not a term used in the legalities associated with cheques.

110 A

An endorsement (signing the cheque on the reverse) is a way of enabling a cheque, not crossed 'account payee only', to be placed in someone else's account. Crossing a cheque limits the use of the cheque. Although it can be endorsed, it should be paid into a bank account rather than being cashed. A cheque guarantee is available up to the limit of a cheque guarantee card, but this is only available between the drawer and the payee and not a third party. A credit transfer is another form of transferring money through the banking system.

111 C

A charge card (e.g. American Express, Diners Club) balance must be paid off in full. Unlike credit cards, no credit facilities are offered. A debit card allows the customer to make payment of a bill electronically from his/her bank account. A cheque guarantee card 'guarantees' a cheque up to the limit of the card, as long as its conditions have been met.

112 D

The amount of a direct debit can be varied and is originated by the recipient (i.e. the company operating the store card in this case). The other forms of transfer are all originated by the bank customer. The standing order is for a fixed amount, until it is changed. Credit and mail transfers are not automatic.

113 D

The drawee is the bank of the person who is making the payment. The person or business paying and signing the cheque is the drawer. The person or business paid is the payee.

114 C

Crossing the cheque means that the cheque cannot be cashed. It must be paid into a bank account. If crossed 'account payee' it must be paid into the account of the payee and no one else.

115 A

Immediate settlement of a debt is possible using a debit card. Payment by a credit card or charge card is from a separate account, which the customer will need to pay off at a later date. Cheques are not immediate.

116 A

The amount of a direct debit can be varied and is originated by the recipient (the utility company in this case). An inter-bank transfer tends to be used for larger amounts, such as the settlement of house purchases. It is not a regular arrangement. A standing order is for a fixed amount, until it is changed. EFTPOS is the name of an electronic transfer systems used for BACS payroll payments to employees, for example.

117 C

A remittance advice details the amount paid. This may be the total of a statement received from a supplier, or simply part of that total. A debit note may be issued if, for example, an invoice is undercast in error. A remittance list accompanies and lists the cheques paid into the bank.

118 B

The originator of the direct debit is able to vary the amount of the direct debit charge each time payment is requested. This is suitable for paying monthly heat and light charges as usage and charges are likely to vary each month. The direct debit authorisation will not contain a specific or fixed amount to be paid.

119 B

The drawer of a cheque is the account holder whose account will be debited when the cheque is presented for payment. The person who is the recipient of the cheque is the payee and the bank in which the cheque is drawn is the drawee.

120 B

The cheque card guarantees cheques up to the limit defined on the cheque guarantee card so long as certain conditions are fulfilled. All the other options offer the facility to make payments directly without the need for a cheque.

121 B

Companies other than banks may issue credit cards. It is important that the retailer accepting the credit card checks that the card is valid and belongs, as far as can be seen, to the person presenting it. These security measures militate against fraud.

122 D

It is a relatively short time in the UK. Because of geographical and other difficulties in other countries it can take longer. More automated and electronic systems can speed up the system.

123 A

Because banks provide a variety of services for customers, all of these relationships are relevant. The main relationship is receivable/payable, because one party always owes the other. The bank acts as agent for the customer when making payment on the customer's behalf. Mortgagor/mortgagee may arise when borrowing. Bailment arises when the bank holds securities and other valuables for the customer, say, in the bank vaults.

124 B

Restoration of the imprest means putting the petty cash balance back to the imprest amount. So, assuming there are no receipts during the period, the amount of cash needed will equal the total of the vouchers.

125 C

The bank provides useful services for the customer, so the customer has to take a degree of care in operating his/her account. The customer is not a salesperson for the bank and there is no reason why a customer should not have more than one account with more than one bank.

126 D

There is less in the till than there should be, because there would have been $250 in the till at the start of the day. According to the cash register, there should have been $1,323.21 in the till at the end of the day.

127 C

A crossed cheque must be paid into a bank account. The further restriction is that the crossing is stated to be "Account payee" which means that it can only be paid into the bank account of the payee, A Smith.

128 D

This ensures that the correct amount is charged to petty cash and the entertainment account.

129 B

130 C

The petty cash withdrawals totalled $62.12 for the month. However, the $53.50 cash added to petty cash from the drinks machine of $53/50 can be offset against the payments made to arrive at a net reimbursement required of only $8.62.

131 C

	$
Cash float on hand	27.18
Add: payments	32.82
Add: unrecorded payment	15.00 – reimburse $32.82 + $15.00 = $47.82
	75.00
Imprest amount	75.00

132 B

All of these represent the items needed to make a payment into the bank. A cheque remittance list may also be used, but it is not a requirement.

133 C

There is no difference because there is a compensating error in both cash and the petty cash records. All the other options lead to a difference in either the cash or the vouchers.

134 C

	$
Sales	193.24
Less: wages	(20.00)
	173.24

135 C

Petty cash is used for small items and for convenience. Larger items, particularly when invoiced, would normally go through the usual channels and be paid by cheque.

136 B

	$
Opening balance	65
Less: payments	(64)
Add: replenished from bank	50
	51

137 C

Although the petty cash is a relatively small amount in comparison with the overall transactions of a business, it should still be held securely.

138 C

It saves invoicing or making out cheques for small amounts.

139 C

The proof of expenditure is linked to receipts and other information received about payments made.

140 D

Any cheque more than six months old may be returned by the customer's bank, so the quickest and most appropriate action is to contact the customer to alter the cheque. 'Correcting' the date could be regarded as fraud. Banks write 'refer to drawer' on cheques when returning them. The supplier would not do this.

141 D

BACS involves electronic payments through the banking system and is suitable for payroll.

142 A

The transactions by cheque, direct debit, standing order and other bank transactions are shown on a bank statement. A statement records the transactions between customer and supplier. Petty cash transactions are included in the petty cash book, but there is no external source of information about the transactions. Statements of the transactions on a company credit card are supplied by the card issuer.

143 A

The checkout operator has no authorisation to grant credit and allow the customer to return later. Neither has the operator the ability to change the limit on a debit card. Having the customer arrested is rather drastic. This could result in bad publicity for the supermarket, especially if a mistake has been made.

144 C

A credit card in excess of its limit and an incorrectly completed cheque are invalid as methods of payment. Barter is a way of swapping one item for another and is only useful in limited circumstances. Cash is always acceptable.

145 B

Authorisation requires evidence and a correctly authorised form requiring a cheque to be sent to the supplier. A receipt would not be seen until after payment has been made and a remittance advice is not drawn up until after the cheque is ready to be sent. At the stage the cheque is drawn, the amount in the bank would not be a major consideration. This would or should have been arranged by senior managers.

146 B

Words, figures, date, drawer and payee details should be correct assuming the input is correct. However, if incorrect details have been input to the accounting package and insufficient controls exist in the business, fraud could occur and cheques could be falsely sent to dummy suppliers whose transactions are fictional. All cheques and forms of payment made by an organisation should be authorised and checked.

147 B

This is a procedure to check the work of cashiers. Regular checks, at unknown intervals, are designed to encourage accuracy and discourage fraud. The correctness of documentation can be assessed elsewhere in the business away from the tills. Performance is also looked at in a more global way, but the 'success' of single tills is generally available by looking at duplicate till rolls or from electronic output generated by modern tills.

148 A

An increase in the petty cash float represents an increase in that asset (a debit) and a reduction in the cash account represents a reduction in that asset (a credit).

149 D

$54 + $36 + $17 − $35 − $20 = $52

150 C

PAYROLL

151 A

	$
Gross wages	9,900
Employer's social security contributions	925
	‾‾‾‾‾
	10,825

Employees' social security contributions and income tax are deductions from gross wages and so are included within the gross wages total of $9,900.

152 A

When an employee is paid on the basis of output, at a rate for each unit or piece produced, the remuneration method is called piecework.

153 C

Ping – 135 × $1.15 = $155.25, minimum $165.00

Shan – 140 × $1.10 = $154.00

20 × $1.15 = $23.00

15 × $1.20 = $18.00

TOTAL $195.00

154 D

An income tax code is associated purely with income tax. It is provided by the tax authorities to assist in the calculation of the income tax liability on earnings.

155 B

Simran – 40 × $6.20 =	$248.00	**Liu** – 35 × $7.40 =	$259.00
5 × $9.30 =	$46.50	6 × $11.10 =	$66.60
3 × $12.40 =	$37.20	7 × $14.80 =	$103.60
TOTAL	$331.70	TOTAL	$429.20

156 A

Aimal – Basic weekly wage	$240.00	**Duha** – Basic weekly wage	$260.00
Bonus 5%	$12.00	Bonus 5%	$13.00
		Production bonus	$40.00
TOTAL	$252.00	TOTAL	$313.00

157 C

	$
Pay for 1st 200 pallets (200 × $2)	400
Pay for next 35 pallets (35 × $3)	105
	——
Gross pay	505
	——

158 B

The income tax deducted is a liability to the taxation authorities. The employer merely collects this tax on behalf of the taxation authorities and will pay it to them periodically. The gross amount of salaries (i.e. including the income tax deducted) is shown as an expense.

159 B

This is usually paid over during the month following collection. (Note: this may vary between and within countries, for example: small business may remit income tax on a quarterly basis.)

160 B

The gross pay comprises net pay and deductions made against gross pay. The employer pays the total plus state benefit contributions incurred by the employer.

161 D

$$\frac{4}{52} \times \$15,000 = \$1,153.85$$

162 B

	$
40 hours at $7	280
6 hours at $10.50	63
	——
	343
	——

163 D

	$
Basic commission $90,000 × 2%	1,800
Expensive items $22,000 × 0.5%	110
Sales over $70,000 ($90,000 – $70,000) × 1%	200
	——
	2,110
	——

164 C

	$
38 hours at $7.50	285.00
6 hours at $7.50 × 1.25	56.25
	————
	341.25
	————

165 B

The payroll function is involved in calculating pay. Management or human resources decide matters such as holidays.

166 C

The other information is useful in determining the performance of employees under different headings.

167 C

Third party authorisation is essential as part of the control process in payroll. Only authorised documents confirming work has been completed should be used as evidence that wages and salaries have been earned and need to be paid.

168 D

The payroll documentation provides all details of the basis for the gross pay and all deductions. Any errors here will just be reflected in the payslip. The latter does not provide details of the basic calculations of gross pay. The tax authorities simply hold details about tax and not the breakdown of pay of individual employees. The employee's manager may be aware of the hours an employee worked or the jobs in which the employee was involved. The manager is unlikely to be aware of technical pay details, such as deductions for tax and social security.

169 B

Drawings are a withdrawal of capital by a business owner. Drawings are not wages or salaries.

SALES AND CREDIT TRANSACTIONS

170 C

The total amount invoiced and receivable includes sales tax.

$500 + (17.5% × $500) = $587.50

171 $5,300

Sales tax

	$		$
Payables/bank (input sales tax)	6,000	Balance b/d	3,400
Bank	2,600	Receivables/bank (output sales tax)	10,500
Balance c/d	5,300		
	13,900		13,900
		Balance b/d	5,300

Sales tax on sales (outputs) = 17.5% × $60,000 = $10,500

Sales tax on purchases (inputs) = (17.5/117.5) × $40,286 = $6,000

172 A

As JKL Co is registered to account for sales tax, that must be included within the gross invoice value. It must be split between the net sale 100/120 × $1,200 = $100 = $1,000 and the sales tax amount 20/120 × $1,200 = $200. Whether or not the customer is registered to account for sales tax is not relevant to how the invoice is accounted for by JKL Co.

173 D

As IOP Co is not registered to account for sales tax, it cannot be included within the value of the sales invoice. Whether or not the customer is registered to account for sales tax is not relevant to how it is accounted for by IOP Co.

174 B

Sales revenue transactions are recorded at values excluding sales tax, as credit entries.

175 C

RTY must separate the sales tax and the net credit note amount to record them in different general ledger accounts. The net credit note value is: 100/110 × $363 = $330 and the sales tax amount is: 10/110 × $363 = $33. Returns inwards relates to goods returned by customers.

176 B

The receivable account should be debited with the full amount payable, including the sales tax. The entry in the sales account should be for the sales value excluding sales tax. Sales tax payable to the tax authorities should be credited to the sales tax account (liability = credit balance).

177 A

	$
List price	1,325.00
Less: trade discount at 20%	265.00
	————
	1,060.00
	————

Sales tax 10% × $1,060.00 = $106.00

178 B

$12,000 × 90% × 15% = $1,620

179 C

This is a sale for payment at a future date. Immediate sales are regarded as cash sales.

180 C

$700 × 95% × 20% = $798

181 B

$414 × 100/115 = $360 credit to sales

182 D

Sales tax is accounted for at the date of sale. At the time of receipt, the only accounting entries required are to record the receipt and reduce the receivable.

183 C

This indicates more sales tax has been paid out than received, so sales tax is recoverable from the tax authorities.

184 D

Receivables

	$		$
Opening balance	4,529	Bank	7,231
Credit sales $16,540 × 60%	9,924	Balance c/d	7,222
	————		————
	14,453		14,453
	————		————

185 D

Receivables

	$		$
Opening balance	5,329	Bank (bal fig)	80,138
Sales ($69,200 × 1.15)	79,580	Closing balance	4,771
	———		———
	84,909		84,909
	———		———

186 B

			$	$
June 12	Sale: list price			5,000
	Less trade discount (25%)			(1,250)
				———
				3,750
June 16	Returns: list price		(1,000)	
	Less trade discount		250	
			———	(750)
				———
				3,000
June 16	Payment (50%)			(1,500)
				———
June 30	Balance owed			1,500
				———

187 B

Settlement discount allowed to a credit customer, when they were not originally expected to take advantage of the discount terms, will be accounted for as a reduction in revenue.

188 C

Vic pays $240 × 0.175 = $42

Fran pays $360 × 0.175 = $63 − 42 input tax on purchase = $21

189 B

Sales tax account

	$		$
Input tax $18,480 × 10/110	1,680	Opening balance b fwd	3,210
Bank payment	2,890	Output tax $21,700 × 10%	2,170
Closing balance c/fwd	810		
	———		———
	5,380		5,380
	———		———

190 A

To reduce overdue balances in the receivables ledger accounts, customers owing money need to be encouraged to pay more promptly. Improved debt collection methods should do this. Allowing credit customers to pay more slowly or giving customers more credit will add to the problems of late payment, not reduce them.

191 B

	$
Sales tax on sales: $1,200 × 20/120	200.00
Less: Sales tax on purchases $810 × 20/120	(135.00)
	65.00

192 B

Output tax represents the sales tax generated from goods and services sold by a business.

193 D

Sales tax account

	$		$
Sales tax on purchases	900	Balance b/d	2,400
Balance c/d	2,750	Sales tax on sales	1,050
		Repayment	200
	3,650		3,650
		Balance b/d	2,750

194 D

The final consumer, who is unable to reclaim the sales tax, pays the tax.

195 B

Sales tax account

	$		$
Input sales tax ($15,200 × 17½%)	2,660	Output sales tax ($24,600 × 17½%)	4,305
Balance c/d	1,645		
	4,305		4,305
		Balance b/d	1,645

196 C

Sales tax account

	$		$
Input tax $30,785 × 17.5/117.5	4,585	Output tax $34,800 × 0.175	6,090
Balance c/d	1,505		
	6,090		6,090

197 C

Sales tax account

	$		$
Input sales tax ($54,200 × 0.175)	9,485	Opening balance	1,354
Balance c/d	2,614	Output sales tax ($72,145 × 17.5/117.5)	10,745
	12,099		12,099

198 A

The invoice determines the tax point from which sales tax is calculated.

199 C

Registration is determined according to limits set by the government.

200 D

Irrecoverable debts are a product of non-payment and time. The longer a debt is outstanding, the less likely it is to be settled. Matters such as insolvency of the receivable also lead to an irrecoverable debt.

201 A

An aged receivables analysis lists the amounts and time invoices are outstanding for named receivables. It is a device used in credit control and receivables are contacted and 'chased' for amounts outstanding longer than the agreed credit period.

202 B

An account which becomes an irrecoverable debt is, initially, an account receivable. So to clear the account, a credit is needed to the account receivable. The other part of the double entry is a debit to irrecoverable debts. At the end of an accounting period, the total of irrecoverable debts is then transferred to the statement of comprehensive income.

203 A

Writing off an irrecoverable (bad) debt is an internal measure which usually follows credit control and legal action. Once it is not cost effective to continue action the account is written off, but the organisation will still hope payment is made at some future time. If a statement is sent, this communicates to the receivable that there is no need to pay.

204 C

Accounts receivable have debit balances. The sum is cleared by the goods returned and the irrecoverable debt written off.

205 D

$500 × 1.2 = $600.00 – i.e. $500.00 + $100 sales tax.

206 C

Sales tax account

	$		$
Input tax 64,200 × 20/120	10,700	Opening balance	4,500
Bank payment	3,600	Output tax $80,000 × 0.20	16,000
Closing balance	6,200		
	———		———
	20,500		20,500
	———		———

207 B

	$
List price	1,480.00
Less: trade discount 5%	(74.00)
	———
	1,406.00
Add: sales tax 20%	281.20
	———
	1,687.20
	———

208 D

	$
List price	10,500.00
Less: trade discount 8%	(840.00)
	———
	9,660.00
Add: sales tax 20%	1,932.00
	———
	11,592.00
	———

209 C

The trade receivables account should account for the full (gross) amount due from the customer. This is calculated as follows: $423.00 × 1.20 = $507.60. This is an amount due to the business; it is a debit balance.

210 D

	$
List price	14,500.00
Less: trade discount 4%	(580.00)
	13,920.00
Less: settlement discount 5%	(696.00)
	13,224.00

211 D

	$
List price	2,800
Less: trade discount 5%	(140)
	2,660
Less: settlement discount 5%	N/A
	2,660

212 B

The write-off of debts will reduce the gross receivables balance by $72,000 to $766,000. The allowance is to be adjusted to $60,000 (hence an adjustment of $12,000).

The net balance is therefore $766,000 less $60,000, i.e. $706,000.

213 D

Trade receivables

	$		$
Balance b/f	10,000	Bank	90,000
Sales	100,000	Irrecoverable in year	800
Irrecoverable debts recovered	1,000	Balance c/f	20,200
	111,000		111,000

214 A

When a debt is written off as irrecoverable, the transaction is recorded as:

Dr Irrecoverable debts account (expense), and Cr Receivables

Any subsequent change to the allowance for receivables should be dealt with as a separate matter.

215 C

Cash sales do not affect receivables. Discounts received affect payables, not receivables. The allowance for receivables does not affect the amount of receivables, but specific irrecoverable debts written off do affect receivables.

Receivables

	$		$
Balance b/f	37,500	Contra with payables	1,750
Sales (credit)	357,500	Irrecoverable debts written off	3,500
		Bank (β)	340,750
		Balance c/f	49,000
	———		———
	395,000		395,000
	———		———

216 B

	$
Irrecoverable debts written off (800 + 550)	1,350
Irrecoverable debt recovered	(350)
Reduction in allowance for receivables	(200)
	———
Charge to statement of profit or loss	800
	———

217 A

Receivables

	$		$
Opening balance b/d	32,750		
Sales	125,000	Bank	122,500
		Payables contra	550
		Sales returns	1,300
		Closing balance	33,400
	———		———
	157,750		157,750
	———		———
Closing balance	33,400		

218 A

Receivables

	$		$
Balance b/d	8,450	Bank	22,430
Sales	19,600	Sales returns	1,000
		Contra	540
		Balance c/d	4,080
	28,050		28,050

219 B

Receivables

	$		$
Balance b/d	500	Credit notes	170
Sales invoices	1,900	Bank (bal fig)	1,530
		Balance c/d	700
	2,400		2,400

220 D

Receivables

	$		$
Balance b/d	54,550	Bank receipts re credit sales	81,622
Credit sales (bal fig)	81,632	Irrecoverable debt w/off	2,000
		Balance c/d	52,560
	136,182		136,182

221 D

	$
List price	250
Less: trade discount 10%	(25)
Add: Sales tax $225 × 1.2	45
Transaction value	270

As this is a credit sale, the output tax on the transaction would have been recorded at the time the invoice was raised. Therefore, the cash receipt is credited in full to the receivables account.

222 A

	$
List price	500
Less: trade discount 10%	(50)
Add; Sales tax $450 × 1.2	45
	———
Transaction value	540
	———

As this is a cash sale, the total receipt must be split between the net sales value and the output sales tax collected. Remember that trade discount is always deducted to arrive at the net sale value of the goods.

223 C

Trade discount is always deducted when calculating the amount invoiced by the seller. In addition, as Smith is not expected to take account of the early settlement discount terms, the amount of revenue receivable is calculated after deduction of trade discount only $950. ($1,000 × 95%). When Smith subsequently pays early to be eligible for the discount, the accounting entries should reflect that fact and record settlement of the amount outstanding and also a reduction in revenue.

Debit Cash $912 ($950 × 96%), Debit Revenue $38 ($950 × 4%), and Credit Trade receivables $950.

224 B

Trade discount is always deducted when calculating the amount invoiced by the seller. In addition, as Jones is expected to take account of the early settlement discount terms, the amount of revenue receivable is calculated after deduction of both trade discount and early settlement discount, a total of $2,280 ($2,500 × 95% × 96%). When Jones subsequently pays early to be eligible for the discount, the accounting entries should reflect the receipt of cash and clearance of the trade receivable for the amount expected.

Debit Cash $2,280 and Credit Trade receivables $2,280.

225 D

Trade discount is always deducted when calculating the amount invoiced by the seller. In addition, as Black is expected to take account of the early settlement discount terms, the amount of revenue receivable is calculated after deduction of both trade discount and early settlement discount, a total of $4,104 ($4,500 × 95% × 96%). When Black subsequently pays outside of the settlement discount period, the full amount of the receivable after trade discount of $4,275 ($4,500 × 95%) is due. The additional cash received in excess of the receivable amount of $171 is therefore accounted for as receipt of additional revenue.

Debit Cash $4,275, Credit Revenue $171, and Credit Trade receivables $4,104.

226 A

Trade discount is always deducted when calculating the amount invoiced by the seller. In addition, as White is not expected to take account of the early settlement discount terms, the amount of revenue receivable is calculated after deduction of trade discount only, a total of $3,515 ($3,700 × 95%). When White subsequently pays outside of the settlement discount period as expected, the full amount of the receivable is due.

227 A

Trade discount is always deducted when calculating the amount invoiced by the seller. In addition, as Green is expected to take account of the early settlement discount terms, the amount of revenue receivable is calculated after deduction of trade discount and early settlement discount, a total of $1,276.80 ($1,400 × 96% × 95%). When Green subsequently pays outside of the settlement discount period, the full amount of $1,344 ($1,400 × 96%) is due and the additional amount received of $67.20 ($1,344.00 – $1,276.80) is accounted for as receipt of additional revenue.

Debit Cash $1,344.00, Credit Revenue $67.20, and Credit Trade receivables $1,276.80.

228 A

The receivable must be removed in full. Therefore, a debit is required to record the cash receipt of $266 and a debit to record the irrecoverable debt of $518, with a credit to receivables account of $784.

229 B

The irrecoverable debt and the increase in the allowance are both written off as part of total expense for irrecoverable debts of $748. As a consequence, receivables will be reduced by $248 and the receivable allowance will be increased by $500.

230 C

The irrecoverable debt expense of $2,160 is reduced by the reduction in the allowance of $350, giving a net expense of $1,810. This expense is matched by an increase in the allowance for receivables and a reduction in the receivables account as follows.

Debit Irrecoverable debts $1,810   Credit Receivables $2,160
Debit Allowance for receivables $350

231 D

The irrecoverable debt expense of $1,888 is increased by the increase in the allowance for receivables of $175, giving a total expense of $2,063. This expense is matched by a reduction I receivables of $1,888 and an increase in the allowance for receivables of $175 as follows:

Debit Irrecoverable debts $2,063   Credit Allowance for receivables $175
                                          Credit Receivables $1,888

PURCHASES AND CREDIT TRANSACTIONS

232 A

Total cost of items purchased, including sales tax = $120 + $60 + $190 = $370.

Sales tax = 17.5/117.5 of this total. $370 × 17.5/117.5 = $55.11.

233 A

The net purchase costs is recorded as a debit entry in the purchases account, and a debit is made to the sales tax account to record the tax element of $42. The payable records the gross amount due to the supplier.

234 C

The purchase return reduces the amount owed to Rawlins Co by $800 plus sales tax.

$800 + (17.5% × $800) = $940.00

235 B

Purchases are recorded excluding sales tax, provided that the business is registered for sales tax.

236 C

The payables account in the general ledger records transactions in total with the suppliers to the business. The balance on the this account is the total amount owed by the business to all its suppliers as at 31 May.

237 B

Sales tax is chargeable on the price after deducting the trade discount of 20%. The full purchase price is therefore 1.175 × $1,600 = $1,880. As the trader is not registered to account for sales tax, the purchases account should be debited with this full amount, including the tax. (A different situation arises when a trader is registered for sales tax.)

238 A

Sales tax on sales = (10/110) × $45,237.50 = $4,112.50

Sales tax on purchases = 10% × $31,500 = $3,150.00

Net amount of sales tax payable (credit balance) = $4,112.50 – $3,150.00 = $962.50

239 A

The payables' account should be debited with the full amount of the purchase return, including the sales tax. The returns outwards account should be credited with the value of the returns excluding the sales tax. The sales tax account should be credited with the amount of tax on the returns (since the tax is no longer recoverable).

240 B

Paying an account payable reduces cash at bank by the amount of the payment and also reduces the total amounts owed to accounts payable, a current liability.

241 A

Returns outwards are purchase returns to suppliers. They can be thought of as 'negative purchases' or 'negative expense', so credit the returns outwards account. The returns reduce the amount owed to payables and debit the payables account (reducing a liability = debit entry).

242 C

The series of transactions might be recorded as follows.

Original purchase

Debit Purchases and Credit payables

On issuing the cheque

Debit payables and Credit Bank

On cancellation of the cheque

Debit Bank and Credit Returns outwards

243 C

The goods are first identified as being needed and then an order is placed. Once the goods are delivered an organisation may find it useful to make out its own form to record receipt of the goods. This is the purpose of the goods received note. This would then be followed by an invoice and possibly a statement. Finally, payment would be made accompanied by a remittance advice.

244 B

Purchases returns are recorded from a credit note and not an invoice.

245 D

The sales tax is determined at the time of sale as opposed to the order.

246 D

The inventory account is used only at the end of an accounting period to record the value of closing inventory. That will become opening inventory at the beginning of the following accounting period.

Purchases are recorded as a debit, and purchases on credit create a payable.

247 D

This indicates the credit period allowed by the supplier.

248 C

Payables

	$		$
Bank	11,583	Opening balance	2,660
Closing balance	3,528	Purchases (bal fig)	12,451
	———		———
	15,111		15,111
	———		———

249 A

Payables

	$		$
Bank ($85,460 – $35,640)	49,820	Opening balance	14,550
Closing balance	12,560	Purchases (bal fig)	47,830
	———		———
	62,380		62,380
	———		———

250 D

Payables

	$		$
Bank (bal fig)	46,289	Opening balance	6,711
Closing balance	6,538	Purchases ($85,400 × 54%)	46,116
	———		———
	52,827		52,827
	———		———

251 B

Payables

	$		$
Bank	29,660	Opening balance (bal fig)	3,819
Closing balance	4,286	Purchases (25,640 × 1.175)	30,127
	———		———
	33,946		33,946
	———		———

252 D

Trade discount is recorded on the invoice and is not recorded in the accounting records of either the supplier or the customer.

253 D

Discounts received reduce the amount a business needs to pay to its supplier.

254 C

The sales invoice is prepared excluding settlement discount as Carlin Co is not expected to take advantage of the settlement discount terms. When Carlin Co does subsequently pay early, Premier Co must account for the receipt of cash and reduction in revenue receivable in order to clear the receivable originally recorded.

255 B

Maycee Co is the purchaser and will record settlement discount received when it makes payment of the invoice within the appropriate time.

256 B

The list of payables includes analysis of amounts outstanding over time. The time element can be monitored closely to ensure that discounts are not missed. As the list is of payables and not receivables, the aged payables analysis is of no value when trying to identify irrecoverable debts.

Other records must be kept to ensure orders are delivered because until an invoice has been issued, an account payable is not created.

257 C

This is a cash transaction as far as the supplier is concerned who receives payment immediately. Therefore, in the accounts of the purchaser, the credit card account replaces bank or cash which are normally used for cash transactions.

258 A

As the types of coding errors are not detailed, A is the most appropriate answer. In a computerised system the accounts always balance. Accounting packages require the double entry to be completed or further transactions cannot be posted. It is not illegal for a business to make mistakes.

259 D

The purchases expense account (a debit balance) should exclude sales tax charged by suppliers. The sales tax is accounted for in a separate sales tax account.

260 C

Sales tax imposed on purchases should be debited to the sales tax account so that it can be offset against sales tax charged by the business on sales.

261 B

Purchase returns represent the cost of goods returned to suppliers. The payables account is debited (the liability is reduced) to reflect the fact that those goods should not be paid for as that they have been returned.

262 A

	$
List price	800.00
Less: trade discount 5%	(40.00)
	760.00
Less: settlement discount 3.5%	(26.60)
Amount paid	733.40

263 C

264 D

265 A

Payables

	$		$
Error (14,576 – 14,756)	180	Opening bal	3,446
Contra – Receivables	392		
Closing bal	2,874		
	3,446		3,446

266 D

Payables

	$		$
Bank re credit purchases	69,500	Balance b/d	23,450
Balance c/d	25,600	Purchases (bal fig)	71,650
	95,100		95,100

267 C

Trade payables

	$		$
Goods returned	1,300	Opening bal	32,750
Bank	122,500	Purchases	125,000
Contra with receivables	1,100		
Closing bal	32,850		
	157,750		157,750

268 B

Trade payables

	$		$
Goods returned	6,500	Opening bal	52,750
Bank	322,500	Purchases	325,000
Discount received	5,250		
Closing bal	43,500		
	377,750		377,750

269 D

Trade payables

	$		$
Goods returned	4,500	Opening bal	34,560
Bank	260,000	Purchases	270,000
Discount received	7,500		
Closing bal	32,560		
	304,560		304,560

270 A

Trade payables

	$		$
Goods returned	3,500	Opening bal	55,555
Bank	390,000	Purchases	395,000
Discount received	6,500		
Closing bal	50,555		
	450,555		450,555

271 A

Trade payables

	$		$
Goods returned	2,500	Opening bal	33,250
Bank	335,500	Purchases	339,850
Discount received	3,350		
Closing bal	31,750		
	373,100		373,100

272 D

Lynx Co is not registered to account for sales tax, so it cannot be separately accounted for.

273 C

90% × $1,000 = $900 is the net purchase price.

The sales tax thereon is 20% × $900 = $180

The gross payable is $1,080

274 B

95% × $2,400 = $2,280 is the net purchase price.

Less 5% early settlement discount is: 95% × $2,280 = $2,166, with discount received of $114.

275 A

95% × $18,000 = $1,710 is the net purchase price.

Add: sales tax of 10% = $1,710 + 171 = $1,881.

The supplier is registered to account for sales tax and this is added to the invoice. Lion Co is not registered to account for sales tax, so cannot account for and reclaim the input tax.

276 D

$1,200 is the purchase price after trade discount.

Add: sales tax of 10% × $1,200 = $1,320 is the gross payable, including sales tax of $120.

The supplier is registered to account for sales tax and this is added to the invoice. Lion Co is not registered to account for sales tax. Tiger Co can account for the input tax as it is also registered for sales tax.

RECONCILIATIONS

277 A

An entry is required in the bank ledger account for all the correct items in the bank statement that have not yet been recorded by the business. These are the items that the business learns about from the bank statement, and should then record in its own accounting records. Such items include bank charges (including overdraft interest) and details of dishonoured cheques. They are also likely to include details of credit transfers, standing orders and direct debit payments.

278 C

Ledger accounts record financial transactions by a business. They are subject to reconciliations and controls.

279 B

	$
Bank ledger account balance (debit, therefore cash in the bank)	25,000
Items not yet on the bank statement:	
Payments to suppliers	3,500
Payments into the account (lodgements)	(3,800)
Bank statement balance	24,700

280 B

	$
Opening balance	(89.93)
Interest	(16.45)
Closing balance	(106.38)

281 C

	$
Overdraft per bank statement	(38,600)
Deposits not yet credited to the account	41,200
	2,600
Cheques paid but not yet presented to the bank	(3,300)
Overdraft per bank ledger account	(700)

282 D

The bank ledger account should be adjusted for items such as standing order payments and bank charges which have not already been recorded. The other items feature in the bank reconciliation statement itself.

283 C

A credit in the bank statement is a debit entry in the bank ledger account.

284 C

	$
Bank ledger balance	148
Bank charges	(10)
Standing order	(25)
	———
Corrected bank ledger	113
	———
Bank ledger	113
Unpresented cheques	125
Outstanding lodgements	(85)
	———
Bank statement	153
	———

285 A

	$
Balance per bank statement	(210)
Less: unpresented cheques	(83)
Add: uncredited lodgements	30
	———
Corrected balance per bank ledger	(263)
	———

286 A

Timing differences between entries being recorded in the bank ledger account until the transactions appear on the bank statement are common.

287 A

Bank ledger

	$		$
Balance b/d	850	Cheques written	1,200
Sales (cash)	230	Balance c/d	1,380
Receivables (remittances)	1,500		
	———		———
	2,580		2,580
	———		———

288 B

		$	$
Balance per bank statement at 1 April			950
Bank statement movements during April	Cheques	(1,600)	
	Deposits	1,900	
			300
Unpresented cheques at 30 April			(210)
Balance per bank ledger at 30 April			1,040

Only the reconciling items at 30 April are relevant in this calculation: any reconciling items at 1 April not included in the 30 April items will have passed through the bank ledger in April.

289 D

Uncredited lodgements are not errors. They result from a timing difference between the recording of receipts in the bank ledger and their appearance on the bank statement. The latter will occur later, so the bank statement will be 'out of date' compared with the bank ledger.

290 C

Large amounts of cash and numerous transactions could easily lead to errors. Regular, frequent reconciliations are essential.

291 B

Discount received would not appear on a bank statement, neither would they affect the balance in the bank ledger.

292 B

Cash would be withdrawn from the bank the same day the cheque has been requisitioned and posted to the bank ledger. The other instances would require time for the cheque to be presented to the drawee bank.

293 A

The running balance should be recorded on the latest counterfoil whenever a transaction occurs affecting the bank statement. The business owner will then instantly know how much is available in the bank.

294 C

Bank charges will be unknown to the business until charges are applied to the bank account and recorded on the bank statement. The business owner is normally advised by letter or receipt of the bank statement.

295 A

A credit card purchase is recorded on a credit card statement. The others reflect relatively modern transfers which appear directly on the bank statement.

296 B

297 C

Pencil Co believes that it owes $150 more than the supplier has stated. With items A, C and D, the result would be that the supplier will state that more is owed, not less, than Pencil Co believes to be the case. If the supplier has recorded discount allowed to Pencil Co, which it has not yet recorded, this will reduce the amount owed by Pencil Co.

298 D

BVC Co apparently owes XCO Co $150 more than the supplier statement identifies. With items, A, C and D the result would be that the supplier will state that you owe more, not less. Item B is the only possible answer, which could explain the situation.

299 A

The numbers of invoices would be checked off against the statement and duplicate numbers should be identified. Errors in calculations and discounts should be identified when checking the invoices against orders. Non-delivery of items would be identified through the use of other records. Any discrepancies and errors would be communicated to the supplier.

300 C

301 D

	Payable ledger $	Supplier statement $
Per question	230	3,980
Cheque 1		(270)
Goods returned 2		(180)
Contra 3		(3,200)
Revised balance	230	330

Difference $100 (330 – 230)

302 B

	Lee's records
	$
Per question	14,500
Unrecorded discount	(150)
	———
Revised balance = supplier statement	14,350
	———

Lee Co believes that the amount owed is $150 more than the supplier has stated. Items A, C and D would result in a different outcome.

303 C

304 B

305 B

	$		$
Balance per payable ledger	260	Balance per supplier's statement	1,650
Cash discount disallowed	80	Less: Goods returned	(270)
		Less: Cash in transit	(830)
	——		——
Adjusted payable ledger	340	Revised balance	250
	——		——

Unreconciled difference = ($340 – $250) = $90

306 C

307 D

308 A

309 C

	$		$
Initial payable ledger balance	180	Balance per supplier statement	1,650
Discount not allowed by supplier	25	Less: Returned goods	(570)
		Less: Cash in transit	(875)
	——		——
Adjusted payable ledger balance	205	Revised balance	205
	——		——

310 D

	$		$
Balance per payable ledger	450	Balance per supplier statement	257
Invoice not yet recorded	60	Less: Cash in transit	(253)
Adjusted payable ledger	510	Revised balance	510

311 A

	$		$
Balance per payable ledger	834	Balance per supplier statement	838
Credit note not yet recorded	(72)	Less: Cash in transit	(76)
Adjusted payable ledger	762	Revised balance	762

PREPARING THE TRIAL BALANCE

312 B

Assets and expenses		Income, liabilities and capital	
	$		$
Cost of sales	458,000	Sales	628,000
General overheads	138,000	Payables	54,000
Cash on deposit	61,000	Capital	86,000
	657,000		768,000
Therefore receivables	111,000		
	768,000		

The value for receivables must make the total debits and credits equal.

313 C

Extracting a trial balance identifies the existence of errors that lead to a difference between total debit balances and total credit balances. The answer is therefore C.

Answer D is not correct. An expense item is a debit entry in an expense account, and an entry in a non-current asset account is also a debit entry. Although there is an error, it would not be revealed by a trial balance. Similarly, with answers A and B, the errors leave total debits and total credits the same.

Note that, in a computerised accounting system, it is not possible to record an unequal value of debits and credits when recording a transaction.

314 D

To correct the error, we need to reduce building repairs expenses (so credit building repairs account) and we need to record the expense as an increase in equipment repairs costs (so debit the equipment repairs account). Answer A contains the correct double entry, but describes the transaction as an error of omission. An error of omission is one where no double entry was made.

315 B

To correct the error, we need to reduce stationery expenses (so credit stationery expense account) and we need to record the expense as an increase in advertising costs (so debit the advertising expense account.

316 D

Carriage outwards is an expense and should be a debit balance.

317 B

Debit bals		Credit bals	
	$		$
Purchases	16,000	Sales	43,000
Equipment	22,000	Overdraft	8,000
Inventory	19,000	Capital	6,000
	57,000		57,000

318 D

Discounts received should be recorded as:

Debit payables, and Credit discounts received.

To correct, we must:

Debit Suspense $200, and Credit Discounts received $200.

319 C

The error you should look for is one where the correction will require an asset to be recorded (debit balance) and the credit entry will clear the suspense account.

Debit: Non-current asset – equip't, and Credit: Suspense.

320 B

Both the payables and receivables ledger accounts will be showing a balance that is $1,425 greater than in should be before accounting for the contra. To reduce the receivables asset balance requires a credit entry and a debit entry is needed to reduce the payables credit balance. When that is done, a further credit to receivables and debit to payables of $1,425 is required to correctly record the contra entry.

321 D

The entry in the bank account (a debit) was recorded correctly, therefore the suspense account must have a credit balance. This is cleared by debiting the suspense account and crediting the rental income account.

322 D

323 A

324 B

325 B

326 C

The trial balance does not guarantee that the general ledger accounts are error-free. There could be duplicated or omitted transactions. There is no legal or regulatory requirement to prepare a trial balance.

327 D

General ledger account balance will be calculated automatically by the accounting system, rather than being a manual task performed by a member of the accounts department, which may lead to errors.

328 A

329 D

330 B

331 C

This is an error of principle because an expense item (motor repairs) has been charged to a non-current asset account.

332 C

The bookkeeper has not yet correctly accounted for the credit entry relating to the receipt from the insurance company. As the expense was originally accounted for as a treated as a van expense, the insurance company receipt should be matched against that. Therefore, debit suspense and credit van repairs to clear the suspense account.

333 A

Income and liabilities are credit balances in the trial balance.

334 B

Assets, expenses and drawings are debit balances in the trial balance.

335 C

This question combines the fact that income and liabilities are credit balances in the trial balance and assets, expenses and drawings are debit balances.

336 B

Compensating errors can be difficult to find because they are often similar, unlinked, numerical errors made when posting to the general ledger in a manual accounting system.

337 B

The sales tax within the gross cost is: 20/120 × $1,500 = $250. This is the amount by which the purchases expense needs to be reduced and the input tax recorded.

338 C

The sales tax within the credit note is: 8/108 × $1,296 = $96. This is the amount by which the preturns outwards previously recorded needs to be reduced and the output tax on the original sale is reduced by the same amount.

339 D

The correct accounting entries to record a contra are:

Debit: Payables (to reduce the liability outstanding), and

Credit: Receivables (to reduce the amount due from credit customers)

The error is the credit posting to the allowance for receivables account instead of the receivables account. Accounting for sales tax is not relevant as that would have been recorded when the original invoices were recorded.

340 D

There is an overstatement of the gross receivable, along with overstatement of sales and output sales tax. The gross adjustment against receivables is for $900 plus sales tax of $90 = $990. Sales is therefore reduced by $900 and output sales tax is reduced by $90.

Section 5

MOCK EXAM QUESTIONS

ANSWER ALL THE QUESTIONS

1   Kew Co has an overdraft of $4,400 at 1 June 20X5. The following four transactions occurred during June. Kew allows its customers up to 60 days to pay its invoices.

3 June   Kew sold goods priced at $10,000 on credit to a customer who always takes the full credit period.

10 June   Kew paid a supplier $8,000.

20 June   Kew made a cash sale of goods with a list price of $12,000 less 5% trade discount.

23 June   Cash was received from a customer who has been in dispute with Kew. The original invoice was for $6,000, but Kew agreed to accept half the invoice value to settle the dispute.

What was Kew's bank balance at 30 June 20X5?

A $2,000

B $2,600

C $10,800

D $12,000

2   Victoria & Co wishes to buy goods from Paddington & Co.

Which of the following is the most likely flow of documents to complete the purchase?

A   Purchase order, delivery note, goods received note, cheque requisition, invoice

B   Purchase order, delivery note, goods received note, invoice, cheque requisition

C   Goods received note, purchase order, delivery note, invoice, cheque requisition

D   Purchase order, goods received note, delivery note, cheque requisition, invoice

3   **Which of the following statements best explains the purpose of the journal?**

    A   It is a record of all transactions included in the general ledger accounts

    B   It is a record of all cash transactions included in the general ledger accounts

    C   It is a record of all credit transactions included in the general ledger accounts

    D   It is a record of transactions included in the general ledger accounts dealing with errors, year-end adjustments and other non-routine transactions

4   **Which of the following is NOT an effective security procedure?**

    A   A key must be inserted in to the cash register before it will operate. Keys are held by authorised personnel

    B   Cash is counted by a responsible person who works on the cash register

    C   The cash reconciliation should be performed by a responsible person who neither operates the cash register nor counts the cash

    D   Cash should be banked as promptly as possible

5   **Which document lists the invoices, credit notes and amounts paid by a business and is issued by a supplier to customers, usually on a monthly basis?**

    A   Delivery note

    B   Purchase order

    C   Quotation

    D   Statement of account

6   Pimlico & Co owes Vauxhall for goods it recently purchased. Pimlico & Co are settling the invoice early and will pay the discounted amount.

    What is the correct double entry for this in Pimlico & Co's accounting records?

    A   Debit Payables, Credit Bank, Credit Discount received

    B   Debit Payables, Debit Discount received, Credit Bank

    C   Debit Bank, Credit Revenue, Credit Payables

    D   Debit Bank, Debit Revenue, Credit Payables

7   The opening balance at 1 June 20X8 on Northolt's receivables' general leger account showed total amounts owed as $6,478. During June Northolt made sales of $53,998, half of these sales were for cash. At 30 June 20X8 Northolt's customers owed $10,492.

    How much cash did Northolt receive from its total sales for the month of June 20X8?

    A $58,012

    B $49,984

    C $31,013

    D $22,985

8 Salah calculated that the bank ledger balance was a debit balance of $230 at 31 December 20X4, but the bank statement balance at that date was a different amount. Items that may affect the bank statement balance at that date were as follows:

(i) A cheque that Salah paid into the bank for $250 was still outstanding

(ii) A cheque for $85 paid by Salah to Jota had not yet been presented at the bank

(iii) Salah had forgotten to record a cash withdrawal of $70

(iv) Salah's bank statement included bank charges of $25 which had been deducted from her account

What was the balance on Salah's bank statement at 31 December 20X4?

A $325

B $65

C $10

D $30

9 **What legislation prevents the unnecessary retention of personal information?**

A Contract law

B Data protection law

C Document retention law

D Sale of goods legislation

10 **Which of the following is an expense for a business which has a large fleet of motor vehicles?**

(i) Purchase of a new delivery van

(ii) Redecorating the transport manager's office

(iii) Paying the road fund licenses for the fleet of vehicles

(iv) Purchase for a new exhaust for a van

A All four expenses

B (ii), (iii) and (iv)

C (i) and (ii)

D (iii) only

11 **What is the purpose of a remittance advice?**

A To pay a supplier

B To remind a customer to pay

C To match a customer's payment with the invoices paid

D To send goods back to a supplier

12 Which of the following will a bank refuse to accept?

A   An unsigned cheque

B   A crossed cheque made out to the person presenting it

C   An account payee cheque paid in by the named person

D   A large deposit of notes and coins

13 What are the accounting entries to record the transfer of surplus petty cash no longer required into the bank account of a business?

A   Dr Bank,   Cr Petty cash

B   Dr Bank,   Cr Sales

C   Dr Sales,   Cr Bank

D   Dr Petty cash,   Cr Bank

14 Which method of payment would be used to make an immediate internet purchase?

A   Cash

B   Cheque

C   Credit card

D   Credit transfer

15 Which of the following is asset expenditure?

A   A debt owed to a supplier

B   A bank loan

C   The purchase cost of a new machine

D   Employee salary costs

16 The following information has been extracted from a trader's wages records for April.

(i)   Employees' pension contributions $783

(ii)   Gross basic wages $10,163

(iii) Income tax $2,150

(iv)   Employer's pension contributions $1,011

What will be the total charge for wages in the final accounts?

A $10,946

B $11,174

C $13,096

D $13,324

17 Which of the following categories of account would you expect to have a debit balance when a trial balance is extracted from the general ledger?

(i) Asset accounts

(ii) Liability accounts

(iii) Income accounts

(iv) Expense accounts

A (i) and (iii)

B (i) and (iv)

C (ii) and (iii)

D (ii) and (iv)

18 The balance on an accounts payable general ledger account at 1 April 20X5 was $18,420. During the month the business made purchases on credit of $27,400. Unpaid payables at 30 April 20X5 were $9,250. During April 20X5 credit notes amounting to $2,610 were received from suppliers.

What payments were made to accounts payables during April 20X5?

A $15,260

B $20,810

C $33,960

D $39,180

19 The entries in an accounts receivable general ledger account were as follows:

Balance brought forward	$3,500
Sales	$250,000
Bank	$225,000
Returns inwards	$2,500
Irrecoverable debts	$3,000

What was the closing balance on the accounts receivable general ledger account?

A $23,000

B $25,500

C $26,000

D $28,000

20 Which of the following documents is used to help identify irrecoverable debts?

A An aged payables analysis

B An aged receivables analysis

C A bank statement

D A supplier statement

21 A business that is registered to account for sales tax purchases goods from a supplier. How would the purchase be recorded in the general ledger?

A   Debit Purchases, Credit Accounts payables, Credit sales tax

B   Debit Purchases, Credit Accounts payables, Debit sales tax

C   Credit Purchases, Debit Accounts payables, Credit sales tax

D   Credit Purchases, Debit Accounts payables, Debit sales tax

22 Which of the following is correct in relation to the trade receivables general ledger account?

(i)   The gross value of goods returned by credit customers is debited to the trade receivables general ledger account.

(ii)   Trade discounts to credit customers are excluded from the trade receivables general ledger account.

(iii) Contras between the trade receivables' and trade payables' general ledger accounts are debited to the trade receivables general ledger account.

A   (i) and (ii) only

B   (i) only

C   (ii) only

D   (ii) and (iii) only

23 A supplier of computer equipment allows its customers to deduct 3% from the invoice amount if they pay within 14 days of the invoice date.

What is this an example of?

A   An irrecoverable debt

B   A trade discount

C   A cash transaction

D   An early settlement discount

24 Mo is a salesperson who is paid according to the number of sales made. Mo's earnings are a percentage of the gross sales.

By what method of remuneration is Mo paid?

A   Bonus

B   Commission

C   Overtime

D   Salary

25 A summary of the transactions of Witney & Co, which is registered to account for sales tax at 17.5%, showed the following for the month of November 20X4:

Outputs of $122,610 (inclusive of sales tax) and Inputs of $78,857 (exclusive of sales tax)

At1 November 20X4, Witney owed sales tax of $7,200 and during November paid $6,800.

What is the balance of sales tax owing at 30 November 20X4?

A $4,461

B $4,861

C $9,000

D $9,400

26 Sam started in business as a sole trader, selling flowers. Sam introduced $2,200 of savings into the business and a car, valued at $750.

What journal entry is required to record the capital introduced?

A   Debit Motor vehicles, Debit Bank, Credit Capital

B   Debit Motor vehicles, Credit Capital, Credit Bank

C   Debit Bank, Credit Motor Vehicles, Credit capital

D   Debit Capital, Credit Motor vehicles, Credit Bank

27 **Which of the following documents would you NOT expect to come across when dealing wlth sales to customers?**

A   Purchase order

B   Delivery note

C   Goods received note

D   Statement

28 **Which of the following should be classified as assets in a business that sells scaffolding equipment?**

A   Bank overdraft

B   Accounts receivable

C   Accounts payable

D   Bank loan

29 **Chris withdraws $300 from the business bank account for petty cash. How should this be recorded in the general ledger?**

A   Debit Bank, Credit Petty cash

B   Debit Petty Cash, credit Bank

C   Debit Petty Cash, credit Capital

D   No record is necessary

30 Sock, a business registered to account for sales tax, purchased goods from a supplier for $6,000 plus sales tax of $1,050. Some of the goods were found to be faulty, and Sock returned one-third of the goods to the supplier. The supplier subsequently issued a credit note for the goods returned.

How should the credit note be recorded by Sock?

A   Debit Payables $2,000, Dr sales tax $350, Cr Purchases returns $2,350

B   Debit Payables $2,350, Cr Purchases returns $2,000, Cr Sales tax $350

C   Debit Purchases returns $2,000, Dr Sales tax $350, Credit Payables $2,350

D   Debit Purchases $2,350, Credit Payables $2,350

31 Which of the following errors could NOT be made using computerised accounts?

A   Error of commission

B   Error of principle

C   Omitting an entire transaction

D   Only completing one half of the double entry to record a transaction

32 What is an accounts receivable ledger?

A   An account for recording total sales

B   An account for recording all transactions with credit customers

C   A set of accounts for recording the transactions with individual credit customers

D   A set of accounts for recording the cash and credit transactions with individual customers

33 What is the double entry required to record credit sales invoices in the general ledger?

A   Debit Bank, Credit Sales

B   Debit Receivables , Credit Sales

C   Debit Bank, Credit Sales

D   Debit Receivables, Credit Bank

34 The following totals appear from a listing of purchase invoices:

Total	Suppliers	Sales tax
$	$	$
5,657	4,865	792

What entry should be posted to the purchases account from the listing?

A   Debit Purchases $4,865

B   Debit Purchases $5,657

C   Credit Purchases $4,865

D   Credit Purchases $5,657

35 For what reason does a business try to ensure a division of duties in the accounts department?

A   To reduce the risk of fraud

B   To prevent individuals from being overworked

C   To make supervision easier

D   To improve the cover for absentees

36 Nova discovered a mistake when recording a sales return transaction in the general ledger. Nova had debited the accounts receivables account and credited the sales returns account.

In which accounting record should the adjustment be recorded before it is included in the general ledger?

A   Sales invoice listing

B   Journal

C   Bank reconciliation

D   Supplier statement reconciliation

37 Which of the following is a secure form of paying salaries in a large organisation?

A   BACS

B   Cash

C   Standing order

D   Direct debit

38 Terry has bought a car on credit for the business. Which components of the accounting equation will change as a result of this transaction?

A   Assets and capital

B   Capital and liabilities

C   Assets and liabilities

D   Assets, capital and liabilities

39 What is the impact upon the net assets of a business when an expense is incurred but not yet paid?

A   The net assets of the business remain unchanged

B   The net assets of the business will be reduced

C   The net assets of the business will be increased

D   It is not possible to determine the impact upon net assets without further information

40 Fork Co offers its credit customers a settlement discount of 5% for payment within 10 days of the invoice date. Fork Co is preparing an invoice for a credit customer who purchased goods with a list price of $1,000. This customer is also eligible for 10% trade discount. It is highly probable that the customer will take advantage of the early settlement terms and pay within 10 days.

What will be the total due on the invoice sent to the customer?

A $1,000

B $900

C $855

D $950

41 **After completing a bank reconciliation, which of the following items could require an entry in the bank ledger account?**

(i)   Credit transfers shown in the bank statement

(ii) Dishonoured cheque

A   Item (i) only

B   Item (ii) only

C   Items (i) and (ii)

D   Neither (i) nor (ii)

42 **Which of the following statements is true?**

A   Cash purchases are credited to the purchases account.

B   Cash sales are debited to the sales account.

C   Settlement discounts received are debited to the trade payables account.

D   Settlement discounts received are credited to the trade payables account.

43 **When reconciling a business bank ledger account with the bank statement, which of the following items could require a subsequent entry in the bank ledger account?**

Errors:

1   Cheques presented after the date of the bank statement

2   A cheque from a customer that has been dishonoured

3   An error by the bank

4   Bank charges

5   Deposits credited after the date of the bank statement

6   Standing order payment entered in the bank statement

A   Items 2, 3, 4 and 6 only

B   Items 1, 2, 5 and 6 only

C   Items 2, 4 and 6 only

D   Items 1, 3 and 5 only

44   Knife Co offers its credit customers a settlement discount of 10% for payment within 10 days of the invoice date. Knife Co is preparing an invoice for a credit customer who has purchased goods for $2,000. This customer is also eligible for 5% trade discount. It is highly probable that the customer will not take advantage of the early settlement terms and pay after 30 days in accordance with normal credit terms.

What will be the total due on the invoice sent to the customer?

A $2,000

B $1,800

C $1,900

D $1,710

45   **In which columns in the trial balance should the following general ledger accounts be included?**

	Purchases	Discount received
A	Debit	Debit
B	Debit	Credit
C	Credit	Debit
D	Credit	Credit

46   Dani is a trainee accountant and prepared the following attempt at a bank reconciliation statement.

	$
Overdraft in the bank statement	43,700
Add: deposits not credited by the bank	52,900
	96,600
Less: outstanding cheques to suppliers	7,800
Overdraft in the bank ledger account	88,800

What is the correct balance on the bank ledger account?

A $88,800 overdraft, as stated

B $17,000 overdraft

C $1,400 overdraft

D $1,400 cash in bank

47 **Which pair of the following account balances would you expect to appear on the same side of a trial balance?**

A Purchases and petty cash

B Office equipment and accounts payable

C Accounts receivables and sales

D Telephone expenses and accounts payable

48 Ali operates an imprest system for petty cash, and the float in petty cash is topped up to $250 at the end of each month.

During April, $25 was paid into petty cash by employees paying for private use of the office photocopier and a cheque for $20 was cashed for an employee out of petty cash. During April, cheques for $340 were drawn by Ali for petty cash.

How much cash was paid out for petty cash expenses during April?

A $295

B $345

C $355

D $385

49 When processing an invoice for the purchase of a new motor, Maxi correctly recorded the payable liability but debited the repairs account, rather than the equipment asset account.

What type of error is this?

A Reversal of entries

B Compensating error

C Error of principle

D Error of commission

50 A business has an opening balance on the sales tax account showing a receivable of $590 and a closing balance also showing a receivable of $460. During the period there were standard rated outputs of $4,200 and standard rated inputs of $6,000 both exclusive of sales tax. The standard rate of sales tax is 17.5%.

How much was the sales tax repayment received during the period?

A $185

B $445

C $1,365

D $1,930

Section 6

MOCK EXAM ANSWERS

MOCK EXAM ANSWERS

1   A

		$
1 June	Opening overdraft	(4,400)
10 June	Pay supplier	(8,000)
20 June	Cash sale ($12,000 less 5%)	11,400
23 June	Cash from customer	3,000
30 June	Closing balance	2,000

2   B

Document	Produced by:
Purchase order	Victoria & Co
Delivery note	Supplier
Goods received note	Victoria & Co
Invoice	Supplier
Cheque requisition	Victoria & Co

3   D

A journal is used to record transactions included in the general ledger accounts dealing with errors, year-end adjustments and other non-routine transactions.

4   B

It is not an effective security procedure for the person who takes the cash from customers to count it at the end of the day. It opens up a possibility of theft/fraud.

5   D

The other documents are used in relation to purchases and sales. The statement of account contains financial transactions.

6   A

For example, if a business pays a supplier's invoice of $1,000 by sending a cheque for $950 and taking a $50 settlement discount, the payment transaction would be recorded as:

Debit: Accounts payable $1,000

Credit: Bank $950

Credit: Discounts received $50

7   B

	$
Opening accounts receivable	6,478
Credit sales in June (50% of $53,998)	26,999
	33,477
Closing accounts receivable	(10,492)
Therefore cash from accounts receivable in June	22,985
Cash from cash sales (50% of $53,998)	26,999
Total cash received from customers	49,984

8   D

The $30 balance is an overdraft balance.

	$		$
Salah's recorded bank balance	230	Updated bank ledger balance	135
Cash withdrawal omitted	(70)	Cheque paid in, not yet cleared	(250)
Bank charges	(25)	Cheque payment to Jota, not yet presented	85
Updated bank ledger balance	135	Bank statement balance	(30)

9   B

This prevents businesses holding personal information without legitimate reason.

10   B

Expenses include redecorating work in buildings, vehicle running costs and repairs and maintenance. Only the purchase of a van is asset expenditure.

11   C

A customer issues a remittance advice with the payment of an invoice. This allows the person receiving the payment to match the payment with the invoice.

12   A

A cheque must be signed by an authorised signatory. Without a signature the cheque is not an authority to pay. The bank may query a large amount of notes if tendered by someone unknown, in case the money had the potential of coming from criminal activity.

13   A

The bank account will increase (debit entry) and petty cash will be reduced (credit entry).

14   C

A credit card enables a purchaser to make an immediate payment on a secure server.

15   C

The debt to the supplier and the bank loan are both liabilities and labour costs are expenses.

16   B

The amount charged to the accounts comprises the gross wages and the employer's pension contributions. Employees' pension contributions and income tax are deducted from the gross basic wages.

17   B

Debit balances relate to asset and expense accounts, and credit balances on liability, income and capital accounts.

18   C

	$
Opening payables balance	18,420
Credit purchases	27,400
	45,820
Credit notes received	(2,610)
	43,210
Closing payables balance	(9,250)
Payments to accounts payable	33,960

19   A

Accounts receivable

	$		$
Balance b/d	3,500	Bank	225,000
Sales	250,000	Sales returns	2,500
		Irrecoverable debts	3,000
		Balance c/d	23,000
	———		———
	253,500		253,500
	———		———

20   B

The aged accounts receivable analysis lists outstanding accounts receivable in terms of amount and length of time outstanding which are useful guides in determining when an outstanding debt becomes an irrecoverable debt.

21   B

For example, if a business purchases an item for $1,000 plus sales tax at $175, the ledger entries should be:

Debit Purchases	$1,000
Debit Sales tax	$175
Credit Accounts payable	$1,175

22   C

Trade discounts should be deducted before the invoice is prepared; therefore, they are excluded from the trade receivables account. The remaining two statements (i) and (iii) are false. The gross value of goods returned inwards by credit customers will be credited (not debited) to the trade receivables account to reduce the balance outstanding. Contras between the trade receivables' and trade payables' accounts are accounted for as follows: Debit Trade payables' general ledger account, Credit Trade receivables' general account.

23   D

A trade discount is a discount agreed at the time the sale is made. Examples are bulk purchase discounts for sales orders above a certain size, and discounts to regular customers. A discount offered for early payment is referred to as a settlement discount or a cash discount.

24   B

Commission is percentage-based remuneration which is designed to motivate success.

25   B

Sales tax account

	$		$
Bank	6,800	Opening balance b/f	7,200
Payables/bank (input tax)	13,800	Receivables/cash (output tax)	18,261
Closing balance c/f	4,861		
	———		———
	25,461		25,461
	———		———
		Balance b/f	4,861

Tax on sales (outputs) = $(17.5/117.5) \times \$122{,}610 = \$18{,}261$.

Tax on purchases = $17.5\% \times \$78{,}857 = \$13{,}800$.

26   A

Debit Motor vehicles	$750
Debit Bank	$2,200
Credit Capital	$2,950

27   C

A goods received note is prepared by the purchaser after the goods have been delivered, for internal use only. The supplier receives a purchase order from the customer, provides a delivery note on delivery of the goods, and might issue periodic statements to customers.

28   B

Accounts receivable are a business asset. Accounts payable, bank overdrafts and bank loans are all liabilities.

29   B

The money is being added to petty cash, therefore debit the petty cash account (asset account). The money is being taken from the bank; therefore reduce the bank balance by crediting the bank account.

30   B

The credit note will include sales tax on the returns – this should be accounted for.

31   D

An error of commission is quite easy to make using a computerised system because an incorrect ledger account code could be selected. The same can be said of an error of principle. It is equally possible to omit items in both manual and computerised systems.

32   C

The accounts receivable ledger is a set of accounts for credit customers, each credit customer having an individual account within the ledger. It is a 'memorandum only' record of transactions and does not form part of the double-entry system.

33   B

Credit sales invoices are recorded in the general ledger as a debit to accounts receivable and a credit to the sales account. Remember that, distinct from the double-entry system in the general ledger, the invoices issued to each individual credit customer are also transferred, as debit entries in the individual accounts of the customers in the receivables ledger.

34   A

The transfer to the purchases account (debit entry for an expense) should exclude sales tax.

35   A

Division of duties means that one person is able to check the work done by someone else. This builds in a control, so that errors and fraud are more easily detected.

36   B

The journal is the record used to record the correction of errors in the accounting records.

37   A

BACS is an electronic system of payment and is far more secure than holding cash on the premises for wages. Standing orders and direct debits are used by customers to pay amounts to suppliers of goods and, more frequently, services.

38   C

The car is an asset and accounts payable are liabilities. There is no impact on profit.

39   B

When an expense is incurred, profit will be reduced, which will result in a reduction in the net assets of the business. This will be reflected in the statement of financial position by inclusion of a liability to reflect the amount still to be paid.

40   C

Trade discount is always deducted prior to the invoice being prepared. Settlement discount is also deducted when it is highly probable that the customer will take advantage of the early settlement discount terms.

	$
Sale price	1,000.00
Less: trade discount (10%)	(100.00)
	————
	900.00
Less: settlement discount (5%)	(45.00)
	————
Invoice amount	855.00

41   C

Credit transfers may not be entered in the bank ledger until they are notified to the business upon receipt of a bank statement. Similarly, dishonoured cheques may not be recorded in the bank ledger account until they are included in a bank statement.

42   C

Settlement discounts received from suppliers are debited to the trade payables account to reduce the remaining balance outstanding to credit suppliers.

43   C

Items shown in the bank statement that should subsequently be recorded in the bank ledger account are items that the business does not learn about until it receives the bank statement. These include bank charges, dishonoured cheques and standing orders and direct debit payments.

44   C

Trade discount is always deducted prior to the invoice being prepared. Settlement discount is only deducted when it is highly probable that the customer will take advantage of the early settlement discount terms. As this customer is not expected to take advantage of the settlement discount terms, settlement discount is not deducted.

	$
Sale price	2,000.00
Less: trade discount (5%)	(100.00)
	————
Invoice amount	1,900.00
	————

45   B

46   D

	$
Bank statement balance	(43,700)
Not yet processed by the bank:	
Cheques from customers	52,900
Cheques to suppliers	(7,800)
Bank ledger account balance	1,400

47   A

Purchases are an expense item and therefore a debit balance. Petty cash is an asset and therefore a debit balance.

48   B

	$
Balance at start of month	250
Payments into petty cash for photocopying	25
Cash to employee	(20)
	255
Cheques drawn for petty cash	340
	595
Balance at end of month	(250)
Therefore petty cash expenditure	345

49   D

50   B

Sales tax account

	$		$
Opening balance	590	Output tax ($4,200 × 0.175)	735
Input tax ($6,000 × 0.175)	1,050	Sales tax repayment (β)	445
		Closing balance	460
	1,640		1,640

Section 7

SPECIMEN EXAM QUESTIONS

Section A – ALL 50 questions are compulsory and MUST be attempted

Each question is worth 2 marks.

1   **Which of the following is an example of capital expenditure?**

    A   Paying for refurbishments as part of upgrading a building

    B   Paying carriage outwards in respect of selling goods

    C   Paying legal fees in order to recover customer debts

    D   Paying bonuses to production operatives

2   Francis maintains a payables account for each supplier. At the end of the period, the account of one supplier showed a credit balance of $15,000. A review of the account revealed two errors:

    1   A purchase invoice for $2,100 was entered in the computerised accounting system as $1,200.

    2   A manual adjustment to the computerised accounting system for a $400 settlement discount received was credited to trade payables and debited to cost of sales.

    What is the adjusted balance on the payables account after the above errors have been corrected?

    A $13,300

    B $15,100

    C $14,900

    D $15,500

3   Christa pays her mortgage by instructing her bank to make monthly payments of a fixed amount from her current account. When the mortgage rate changes Christa issues a revised instruction to the bank.

    Which method of payment is Christa using?

    A   Standing Order

    B   Credit card

    C   Direct Debit

    D   Cheque

4   A manual adjustment of Dr Trade Receivables and Cr Sales has been made in the computerised accounting system to recognise a sale totalling $480,000. This amount of $480,000 includes, incorrectly, sales tax at 20%.

What is the sales figure that should be included in the trial balance?

A $480,000

B $384,000

C $400,000

D $576,000

5   Which of the following would be on the credit side of the receivables control account?

1   Cash received

2   Irrecoverable debts

3   Credit notes issued

4   Credit sales

A   1, 2 and 3 only

B   2 and 4 only

C   1 and 4 only

D   1, 2, 3 and 4

6   The following is a summary of the petty cash transactions for a week:

Income	$	Expenditure	$
Opening balance	500	Travelling expenses	150
Sale of stamps	10	Subsistence expenses	250
Sale of paper	50		

Petty cash is maintained using the imprest system.

What sum should be reclaimed by the cashier at the end of the week?

A $160

B $340

C $400

D $500

7   The balance on the trade payables ledger account should be equal to which other figure in the accounting system?

A   The total of the balances on the individual customers' accounts

B   The total of the balances on the individual suppliers' accounts

C   The balance on the trade receivables general ledger account

D   The balance on the purchases general ledger account

8   Louise introduces her car into her business.

Which parts of the business' accounting equation will change?

A   Assets and capital

B   Capital and profit

C   Liabilities and assets

D   Capital and liabilities

9   Freya started in business on 1 September. During September she made cash sales of $6,400 and issued credit sales invoices for $10,200 of which $8,600 has since been paid.

What would be the balance of the sales account in the general ledger at the end of September?

A $6,400

B $10,200

C $8,000

D $16,600

10   **Which of the following journal entries correctly records the credit purchase of plant and equipment?**

A   Dr Trade payables   Cr Plant and Equipment

B   Dr Cash   Cr Plant and Equipment

C   Dr Plant and Equipment   Cr Trade payables

D   Dr Plant and Equipment   Cr Cash

11   Ted is preparing his bank reconciliation. Ted's bank statement for July shows that he is overdrawn by $150. Ted has been notified of a bank error: the bank has taken $50 from his account in error and this has not yet been corrected. Ted has deposited cheques for $380 which are not yet showing on his bank statement.

What is the balance on Ted's bank ledger account?

A $180 credit

B $480 credit

C $280 debit

D $580 debit

12 Albert sold 15 units of inventory with a list price of $40 per unit to Michael. He gives Michael a 10% trade discount and also a 5% settlement discount if Michael pays within 30 days. Based upon previous experience, Michael never pays early to take advantage of settlement discount offered.

What will be the total of the invoice that Albert issues to Michael for this transaction?

A $540

B $600

C $510

D $513

13 Jess is preparing her trial balance. Jess's balanced off trade receivables ledger account is shown below.

Trade receivables

	$		$
Balance b/d	500		
Sales	1,150	Cash	1,250
		Balance c/d	400
	1,650		1,650

What amount should be shown for trade receivables in Jess's trial balance?

A $400 credit

B $400 debit

C $1,650 debit

D $1,650 credit

14 Wendy is in the process of preparing a bank reconciliation for her business.

Which of these statements is not correct?

A   Bank charges should be credited in the bank ledger account

B   Unpresented cheques should be deducted from the bank statement balance in the bank reconciliation

C   Direct debit and standing order payments should be credited in the bank ledger account

D   Dishonoured cheques from customers should be debited in the bank ledger account

15   Which of the following are potential benefits of an effective document retention policy to a small business?

1   To ensure all documents are stored forever

2   To meet legal and tax requirements of the business

3   To mitigate risks arising from internal and external disputes of the business

4   To increase operational efficiency and maintain control over costs

A   1 and 3 only

B   2, 3 and 4 only

C   1, 2 and 4 only

D   1, 2, 3 and 4

16   Hywel purchased goods on credit with a list price of $100. The supplier gave Hywel a trade discount of 10%. Sales tax is charged at 20% and both Hywel and the supplier are registered for sales tax.

What is the amount that Hywel will debit to his purchases account?

A $88.00

B $90.00

C $108.00

D $110.00

17   On 15 March 20X5 Trevor makes the following purchase from credit suppliers:

1   A purchase from Anneke of goods with a list price of $4,000. Because Trevor is a regular customer, Anneke gives Trevor a 10% trade discount.

2   A purchase from Basil of goods with a list price of $6,000 with a 2% discount if Trevor pays within 7 days. Trevor is not expecting to pay within the 7-day period.

What is the value of purchases to be recorded on 15 March 20X5?

A $9,480

B $9,600

C $9,880

D $10,000

18   A credit sale of goods for $51 to J Davis was entered in the accounts as $15.

What type of error has occurred?

A   Compensating error

B   Error of omission

C   Error of principle

D   Error of transposition

19 Which of the following represents the correct imprest amount in an imprest petty cash system?

A   Notes and coins in the cash box – vouchers for payments – IOUs

B   Notes and coins in the cash box + vouchers for payments – IOUs

C   Notes and coins in the cash box – vouchers for payments + IOUs

D   Notes and coins in the cash box + vouchers for payments + IOUs

20 Which of the following statements are true about a good coding system for financial transactions?

1   It enables a company to easily extract data for management analysis

2   It provides a unique code for each item within the system

3   It provides codes that are uniform in format

4   It requires management authorisation before creation of new codes

A   1 and 2 only

B   3 and 4 only

C   2, 3 and 4 only

D   1, 2, 3 and 4

21 Raoul uses the following codes in his accounting system.

Payables system	
Suppliers	**Supplier code**
Smith A F	3451
Smythe A	3452
General ledger	
First number	**Second number**
100 = Income	500 = Rent
200 = Expense	600 = Electricity

Raoul received an invoice from A. Smythe, a supplier, for the rent of an office.

How should the invoice from A. Smythe be coded for input into Raoul's accounting system?

A   Supplier code: 3451   General ledger code: 100500

B   Supplier code: 3451   General ledger code: 200500

C   Supplier code: 3452   General ledger code: 200500

D   Supplier code: 3452   General ledger code: 100500

22 Annabel's bank ledger shows her to be $2,030 overdrawn. A bank reconciliation, however, shows that a standing order payment for $365 had been entered in the bank ledger twice, and that a manual journal entry meant for recognising a $275 petty cash payment was wrongly debited in the bank ledger account.

What is Annabel's corrected overdraft balance?

A $1,845

B $1,940

C $1,850

D $2,215

23 Narvinda buys goods from Jamal for $2,500. He returns half of the goods on 15 May.

Which of the following documents would be issued by Jamal for the return of the goods?

A   Invoice

B   Credit note

C   Debit note

D   Remittance advice

24 Alexia has taken out a new bank loan which requires monthly payments of a variable amount to be paid from her current account.

Which method of payment would be best for Alexia to use?

A   Payable order

B   Crossed cheque

C   Direct debit

D   Standing order

25 **Which of the following statements about coding are correct?**

1   Each general ledger account within an accounting system has a unique code.

2   If an invoice is posted using the wrong code in the payables ledger, it will be credited to the wrong supplier account.

3   If two customers have the same name, they will also have the same code in the receivables ledger.

4   Customer account numbers are an example of coding used in an accounting system.

A   1, 2 and 3 only

B   1 and 4 only

C   1, 2 and 4 only

D   2 and 3 only

26 A credit entry into a ledger account represents which of the following?

    A   Increase in an expense

    B   Increase in income

    C   Increase in an asset

    D   Increase in drawings

27 Iwan's trade payables ledger account showed that $2,300 was owed to suppliers at the start of the week. During the week Iwan made purchases of $3,900 although he paid $900 of this in cash. He also paid suppliers $1,000 through an electronic bank transfer.

    What is the closing balance on his trade payables ledger account?

    A $4,000

    B $4,300

    C $5,200

    D $6,100

28 Which of the following statements regarding the journal entries is NOT correct?

    A   A journal entry can be used to make transfers between general ledger accounts

    B   A journal entry should only be used to make corrections to the general ledger due to errors

    C   A journal entry must always contain equal debit and credit entries

    D   A journal entry should include a narrative explanation

29 What document is usually sent every month from the supplier to the customer, listing all the transactions between them during that month?

    A   Invoice

    B   Receipt

    C   Statement of account

    D   Credit note

30 A company has the following year end payroll information

Gross salaries and wages	$285,350
Income tax deducted	$61,063
Employers' pension contributions	$26,786
Employees' pension contributions	$23,034

    What is the company's total payroll cost for the year?

    A $312,136

    B $274,107

    C $396,233

    D $308,384

31 Walter sells goods to Ninevah with a list price (exclusive of sales tax) of $4,300, offering a 4% trade discount. Walter is registered to account for sales tax and the rate of sales tax is 17.5%

What amount should be recorded for this transaction in Walter's sales account (to the nearest $1)?

A $4,850

B $4,128

C $5,053

D $3,513

32 Which of the following statements regarding sales tax in the trial balance is true?

A Output tax and input tax are debit balances

B Output tax and input tax are credit balances

C Output tax is a credit balance and input tax is a debit balance

D Output tax is a debit balance and input tax is a credit balance

33 Which of the following should be classified as current liabilities?

1 Trade receivables

2 Sales tax payable

3 Trade payables

4 Drawings

A 1 and 2

B 2 and 3

C 3 and 4

D 2 and 4

34 Sally's bank ledger account balance is $160 debit. However her bank statement shows a different amount. On investigation, Sally discovered the following:

1 A cheque that Sally paid into the bank for $40 is still outstanding.

2 A cheque for $60 paid by Sally to Molly has not yet been presented.

3 Sally has forgotten to record a cash withdrawal of $30.

4 The bank has deducted charges of $15 from her account which have not been reflected in the bank ledger account.

What is the balance on Sally's bank statement?

A $95

B $135

C $185

D $225

35 Avalon gives his customers individual trade discounts from the list price and also offers a 5% early settlement discount for all invoices settled within seven days of issue. A new customer, Novala, negotiated a 25% trade discount. Novala is not expected to take advantage of the settlement discount terms offered. Novala's transactions during June were:

12 June   Bought goods with a $5,000 list price

15 June   Returned goods with a $1,000 list price as faulty

16 June   Paid half of the net balance on its account

How much does Nolava owe Avalon at 30 June?

A $1,425

B $1,500

C $2,000

D $2,850

36 Richard has a balance of $350,000 on his trade payables ledger control account at the end of May.

What does this mean?

A   He has bought $350,000 of goods in May

B   He is owed $350,000 by his customers

C   He owes $350,000 to his suppliers

D   He has paid $350,000 to his suppliers in May

37 **Which of the following statements about a computerised accounting system are correct?**

1   It can be used to produced reports required by management, such as a sales analysis report.

2   It removes the need for journal entries to be used.

3   It may link directly with other systems in the business.

4   It does not require the business to use a coding system as transactions are recorded automatically.

A   1 and 3

B   1 and 4

C   2 and 4

D   2 and 3

38 Seb packs goods on an assembly line. He is paid a different amount each week, depending on his output of assembled goods.

By what method of remuneration is Seb paid?

A Piecework

B Commission

C Hourly rate

D Salaried

39 The following ledger balances make up a company's trial balance:

	$
Sales	76,700
Purchases	26,800
Non-current assets	31,400
Trade payables	18,200
Trade receivables	32,300
Cash at bank	14,200
Capital	9,800

What is the total of the debit column of the trial balance?

A $94,900

B $104,700

C $105,900

D $209,400

40 Susan is a computer equipment dealer. She uses the following coding system for her financial transactions:

1st number	2nd number
100 Purchases	300 Cash
200 Sales	400 Trade payables
	500 Trade receivables

Danielle buys computer equipment worth $2,000 on credit from Susan.

Which of the following would be the code recorded on the invoice issued by Susan?

A 100300

B 100400

C 200300

D 200500

41 Katrina's trade payables account is shown below:

Trade payables

	$		$
Cash	2,900	Balance b/d	750
		Purchases	3,500

Which of the following shows the correct way to balance off Katarina's trade payables account?

A   **Trade payables**

	$		$
Cash	2,900	Balance b/d	750
Balance c/d	1,350	Purchases	3,500
	4,250		4,250
		Balance b/d	1,350

B   **Trade payables**

	$		$
Cash	2,900	Balance b/d	750
		Purchases	3,500
	2,900		4,250
Balance b/d	1,350		

C   **Trade payables**

	$		$
Cash	2,900	Balance b/d	750
		Purchases	3,500
	4,250		4,250
		Balance b/d	4,250

D   **Trade payables**

	$		$
Cash	2,900	Balance b/d	750
		Purchases	3,500
	2,900		4,250
		Balance b/d	1,350

42 Jenny has a bank balance of $550 at the start of the week. During the week the following transactions occurred:

Day 1   She sold goods on credit for $876

Day 2   She received a cheque for $400 from a credit customer

Day 3   She purchased office equipment with a list price of $1,000 but received a 10% discount for paying immediately by cheque

Which of the following items will appear as a credit balance in the general ledger?

A   Sales tax refund owed from tax authorities

B   Petty cash

C   Purchase returns

D   Sales returns

43 **Which of the following correctly shows the accounting equation?**

A   Assets − Liabilities = Opening capital − Profit − Drawings

B   Assets = Opening capital + Profit + Drawings − Liabilities

C   Assets + Liabilities = Opening capital + Profit − Drawings

D   Assets = Opening capital + Profit − Drawings + Liabilities

44 Vauxhall recently sold goods on credit to Pimlico. Vauxhall does not expect Pimlico to take advantage of settlement discount offered for early payment of the invoice. However, Pimlico subsequently does pay early and is entitled to pay the reduced amount.

What is the correct double entry for settlement of the amount due in Vauxhall's accounting system?

A   Dr Trade payables Cr Bank   Cr Discount received

B   Dr Trade payables Dr Discount received   Cr Bank

C   Dr Bank   Cr Sales   Cr Trade receivables

D   Dr Bank   Dr Sales   Cr Trade receivables

45 Fred works on a car factory assembly line and is paid a rate of $4.50/hour for a 35 hour week. All overtime is paid at time and a half. In addition a piecework rate of $25 for every car assembled each week is paid.

Last week Fred worked 46 hours and completed the assembly of three cars.

How much is Fred's gross pay for the week?

A $282.00

B $256.75

C $306.75

D $385.50

46 A sale is made to a credit customer with a list price of $4,500 net of sales tax. As the customer buys frequently from the business a trade discount of 5% is offered. Sales tax is charged at 20%.

What is the amount of sales tax charged on this transaction?

A $900

B $750

C $855

D $713

47 Carion sells the following goods for cash during January:

		Net Price	Sales Tax
		$	$
5 Jan	To Maurice	386	68
19 Jan	To Harris	715	125
28 Jan	To Merton	430	75

What are the following journal entries could correctly account for these sales?

A   Dr Sales $1,799   Dr Sales tax $268   Cr Cash $2,067

B   Dr Cash $2,067   Cr Sales $1,799   Cr Sales tax $268

C   Dr Sales $1,531   Dr Sales tax $268   Cr Cash $1,799

D   Dr Cash $1,799   Cr Sales $1,531   Cr Sales tax $268

48 **What journal entry would be posted if a sole trader starts a business by introducing cash savings and a car into the business?**

A   Dr Motor vehicles   Dr Bank   Cr Capital

B   Dr Bank   Cr Motor vehicles   Cr Bank

C   Dr Capital   Cr Motor vehicles   Cr Bank

D   Dr Motor vehicles   Cr Capital   Cr Bank

49 Malindra sent a payment to Nicholas along with a document detailing the items and invoices the payment related to.

What is this document known as?

A   Debit note

B   Credit note

C   Remittance advice

D   Delivery note

50 The following statements relate to the receivables ledger account:

1 Settlement discounts received will not be recorded in the trade receivables ledger account.

2 The allowance for the irrecoverable debts is recorded in the trade receivables ledger account.

Which of the above statements are true?

A 1 only

B 2 only

C Both 1 and 2

D Neither 1 nor 2

(Total: 100 marks)

Section 8

ANSWERS TO SPECIMEN EXAM QUESTIONS

1   A

2   B

3   A

4   C

5   A

6   B

($250 + 150 − (50 + 10)

7   B

8   A

9   D

($10,200 + 6,400)

10   C

11   C

12   A

($15 × 40) − (10% of 600)

As settlement discount is unlikely to be taken by Michael, this is ignored when the sales invoice is prepared.

13 B

14 D

15 B

16 B

($100 – 10% of 100)

Only the net purchase cost is debited to the purchases account. The sales tax charged on the purchase invoice will be debited to the sales tax account. The gross amount is credited to the payables ledger control account.

17 B

18 D

19 D

20 D

21 C

22 D

(– $2,030 – $550 + $365)

23 B

24 C

25 C

26 B

27 B

($2,300 + $3,000 – $1,000)

28 B

29 C

30 A

($285,350 + $26,786)

31 B

($4,300 – 4% of 4,300)

32 C

33 B

34 B

($160 – $40 + $60 – $30 – $15)

35 B

½ of ($4,000 – 25% of $4,000)

36 C

37 A

38 A

39 B

($26,800 + $31,400 + $32,300 + $14,200)

40 D

41 A

42 C

($950 – $(1,000 – 10% of 1,000))

43 D

44 D

As Pimlico was not expected to take advantage of the settlement discount offered, initial recording of the sale and receivable is not adjusted for settlement discount. When early settlement is subsequently made by Pimlico, the receivable in Vauxhall's general ledger is cleared by the receipt of cash and a reduction in revenue.

45 **C**

($4.50 × 35) + ($6.75 × 11) + (3 × $25)

46 **C**

47 **D**

48 **A**

49 **C**

50 **D**

Settlement discount received is recorded in the trade payables ledger control account. The allowance for receivables is maintained in a separate general ledger account. It is not part of the trade receivables ledger control account.